TELEVISION
and Sex Role Stereotyping

TELEVISION
and Sex Role Stereotyping

Barrie Gunter

Research Officer
Independent Broadcasting Authority

 John Libbey
LONDON · PARIS

British Library Cataloguing in Publication Data
Gunter, Barrie
  Television and sex role stereotyping. —
  (IBA research monograph)
  1. Sex roles — Public opinion 2. Sex in television
  3. Television — Social aspects
  I. Title   II. Series

  305.3   HQ1075

  ISBN 0-86196-095-5
  ISBN 0-86196-098-X Pbk

Published by
John Libbey & Company Ltd
80/84 Bondway, London SW8 1SF, England (01) 582 5266
John Libbey Eurotext Ltd
6 rue Blanche, 92120 Montrouge, France (1) 47 35 85 52

Typesetting in Rockwell by E E Owens & Co Ltd, London SE15 4AZ
Printed in Great Britain by Whitstable Litho Ltd, Whitstable, Kent

Contents

Chapter 1

Introduction

A fundamental aspect of human social development involves learning to behave in ways deemed socially and culturally appropriate for one's own sex. This socio-cultural normalising of displayed, acceptable characteristics and behavioural roles for males and females has been found to develop among children at an early age (Fauls and Smith, 1956) and may influence a child's choice of activities as early as nursery school (Fagot and Patterson, 1969). Spence, Helmreich and Stapp (1975) demonstrated that stereotyped beliefs were significant factors affecting how people perceived themselves and have an effect particularly on levels of personal self-esteem.

With the emergence of the women's rights movement, sex-role stereotyping has been identified as a source of restrictive practices which limit the number and range of roles, opportunities and prospects open to women socially and more especially in professional and occupational spheres. One argument is that the acceptance of women into certain professional roles is restricted to a significant degree by prevailing stereotypes and images of women in society.

The observation of male and female models in the child's environment has been postulated as a major source of sex-role information (Kohlberg, 1966; Mischel, 1970). The developing child has two principal sources of models — the home and school environments and the mass media and chiefly the audio-visual media. Research which has examined the way the sexes are portrayed on television has noted a pronounced stereotyping of women in adult daytime, peak-time and children's programming and in advertisements (see Butler and Paisley, 1980; Cathey-Calvert, 1983; Durkin, 1985a). This has led writers interested in the elimination of sex stereotypes to request an enforced balance in the portrayal of social and occupational roles which have traditionally been presented as exclusively or predominantly associated with one or other sex (Busby, 1975).

According to the conclusions of this work, stereotyping has been characterised by two principal features: firstly, there is a gross under-representation of women in action-drama programmes in terms of actual numbers relative to the presence of men, something which has been referred to by one writer as the 'symbolic annihilation of women' (Tuchman, 1978). Secondly, even when women do appear, they tend to be portrayed only in a very narrow range of roles. In television's fictional life, women tend to be most often found in the home, and much less often at work. Television has also been accused of portraying women as incompetent, especially when they appear in anything other than marital or familial roles. American researchers have observed that this is reflected particularly in the extent to which female characters in American peak-time television are on the receiving end of violent attacks. One major series of US research studies has indicated that whenever women in television drama programmes are involved in violence, they are more likely than men to be helpless victims (Gerbner, 1972; Gerbner and Gross, 1976; Signorielli, 1984). Thus, Tuchman (1978) has argued that television plots symbolically denigrate women, so that even when they are portrayed in leading roles and outside the home, they are surrounded and continually rescued by male colleagues.

The serious implication of this apparent tendency towards sex-role stereotyping on television lies with the possible impact this content may have on the public's beliefs about men and women. The greatest concern is for the effects on young children at the stage when they are just beginning to learn sex-appropriate attitudes and behaviours. Several studies have indicated that a heavy diet of television viewing at an early age is associated with exaggerated stereotyping of sex role beliefs among boys and girls (Beuf, 1974; Frueh and McGhee, 1975; McGhee and Frueh 1980; Morgan, 1980). This and other research is examined in this monograph to see what evidence there is for an influence of television on people's beliefs about the sexes.

The research will be reviewed in four parts. The first part will look at the characteristics of female and male portrayals on television programmes and advertisements directed both at adults and children. The second part will examine viewers' perceptions of the way women and men are shown on television and the extent to which people make distinctions between the sexes as depicted on television and as they are seen to be in real life. The third part will view research evidence on the effects of television portrayals on sex-role stereotyping. And the fourth part will consider the potential of television as an educational medium for changing sex-role perceptions and reducing stereotyping.

Chapter 2

Portrayal of the sexes on television

According to the results of investigations of television content over the last three decades there is good reason to be concerned about the kind of impact television portrayals might have on what people think about the sexes. Monitoring projects since the mid-1950s have indicated that the portrayal of men and women on television drama is monotonously stereotypic. The accumulated evidence from numerous content analyses has strongly suggested that portrayals of women on peak-time television tend to be unfavourable and lack balance relative to depictions of men both in terms of the frequency with which female characters appear and in the nature of the roles to which they are allocated. We shall look first at evidence on the *frequency* and *nature* of appearances by women on adult television. Then, we shall consider similar evidence for children's programmes, before finally turning to research on sex-role portrayals in television advertising.

Adults' programmes

Most content analyses have focused on soap-operas and action-drama series broadcast at peak-viewing times, although there have been a few studies of daytime programmes, quiz shows and news and public affairs programmes. One of the major issues throughout this research has concerned the frequency with which women are shown on television. Typically, the major finding is that women are seen much less often than men, though there are variations across programme types. Even during the formative years of popular television in the United States, for example, several investigators in that country noted a gross under-representation of women as major characters in programmes (Head, 1956; Smythe, 1954).

Head analysed thirteen weeks of prime-time programming from the major American television networks in 1952, while Smythe examined programmes broadcast during one week by seven television channels in New York over three consecutive years (1951, 1952 and 1953). Both studies revealed that only one-third of leading characters were female. Subsequently, similar general patterns of the numerical prevalence of male and female characters on American network television were recorded by a number of independent workers in this field during the 1960s, 1970s and into the beginning of the 1980s.

Many content analytic studies since have indicated that not only does television portray women less often than men, but more especially women are seen much less frequently in central dramatic roles. In an analysis of US prime-time network dramatic programming aired during the 1969 to 1972 seasons, Tedesco (1974) found that on average only 28 percent of all major roles were played by women. Several further studies during the first half of the 1970s corroborated this finding. In a study of a sample of output from the local television station during 1972, Cantor (1973) reported a 70:30 ratio of male to female fictional characters. Similar ratios were reported by Turow (1974) and Miles (1975). In a subsequent content analysis which covered both dramatic and other types of television programming, O'Kelly and Bloomquest (1976) found a lesser, though still pronounced, two-thirds to one-third numerical bias in favour of males. Rather more promising news for women emerged from a study of female appearances on US television spanning nearly ten years of output. Seggar, Hafen and Hannonen-Gladden (1981) monitored dramas, movies and situation comedies broadcast during five-week periods in 1971, 1973, 1975, and 1980. In terms of actual numbers of appearances and percentages of all portrayals, the presence of women on television drama increased across the decade. Around one in five portrayals were female in 1971 compared to nearly one in three by 1980. Furthermore, increased female presence was most marked in major roles.

The most extensive long-term analysis of television drama content is that routinely conducted each year on prime-time American network television output by Gerbner and his colleagues. From 1967 to 1972 Gerbner (1972; Gerbner and Gross, 1976) noted that women accounted for only one-quarter of all leading characters. From the same research group, more recently, Signorielli (1984) reported that from 1969 to 1981 women were generally outnumbered by men by about three to one and that actual year-to-year fluctuations were very slight.

Female presence and programme type. Whilst television generally appears to be characterised by a gross under-representation of females, the visibility of women on television does seem to vary across programme types. Whilst men certainly dominate in terms of frequency of occurrence throughout most kinds of programmes, the numerical imbalance between male and female characters was observed in some studies to be far less pronounced in, for example, soap-operas and situation comedies than in action-adventure programmes (e.g., crime-detective series and westerns).

Women in action, comedy and soaps. In dramatic American television content as a whole during the mid-1970s, Miles (1975) noted that 39 percent of major characters were women. However, when action-adventure programmes were analysed in isolation, the disparity between the sexes was much greater; only 15 percent of leading characters were women. Meanwhile in situation comedies, nearly equal proportions of male and female characters were recorded.

This pattern of differential presence of the sexes according to programme type was reinforced by the observations of Miller and Reeves (1976). This content analysis of one week's prime-time television drama output on the American networks indicated that males outnumbered females in both major and supporting roles, but that female characters more closely approached males in frequency of appearance in family dramas (soap operas) and situation comedies.

With regard to situation comedy programming, American data have produced varying estimates of the relative numerical bias of men to women. Miles (1975) and Miller and Reeves (1976) reported much reduced numerical imbalances in favour of men, whilst in her longitudinal content analysis stretching from the end of the 1960s to the early 1980s, Signorielli (1984) found that even in situation comedies men generally outnumbered women by two to one. A similar ratio was observed for American comedy programmes by Barcus (1983).

Numerically and on balance, the research indicates that women in televised fiction seem to get the best deal in soap operas. Such programmes are populated almost equally by women and men (Katzman, 1972; Downing, 1974; Turner, 1974). Downing reported that 50 percent of the characters in soap operas she studied were female. Whilst they are more visible in soaps, however, many writers have argued that even here the range of roles female characters are given tends to be very narrow and emphasises certain stereotyped characteristics of the female sex (Butler and Paisley, 1980; Tuchman, 1978).

Characteristics of women on adult programmes. Focusing on the attributes of women on television therefore, it seems that sex-role stereotyping is woven more deeply into the fabric of television programming than the obvious numerical discrepancy between the sexes suggests. Following frequency counts of the distribu]tion of women in different types of role in television drama, a number of basic and recurring characteristics of female portrayals have been identified. 'Propositions' about the nature of a woman's role in life have been formulated which have been assumed to represent messages directly conveyed by television to the public about women. It has been further argued that such 'propositions' are learned by television audiences, thus cultivating a distorted common public consciousness about men and women in reality (Paisley and Butler, 1980; Tuchman, Daniels and Benet, 1978). Sex stereotyping on television has been identified to occur in relation to the kinds of roles in which women and men are portrayed and in connection with the personality attributes they typically display. Stereotyping therefore divides neatly into two types: *sex-role* stereotyping and *sex-trait* stereotyping.

Sex-role stereotyping. Societal attitudes towards which roles are most appropriate for women have been undergoing great changes. In particular, there have been changes in beliefs about the value of the family, the manner in which child care can best be implemented, the role of marriage in people's lives today, and the possibility of self-fulfilment through work.

Changes have occurred in the traditional housewife role which have given many women more time and cultivated needs for activities outside the home and more money. Modern domestic appliances, manufactured goods and prepared foods among other things, save on time and labour. Also, women are having fewer children and often delay having any for the first few years of marriage — so they spend fewer years occupied with child care. Nevertheless, this is apparently not the image of the contemporary woman portrayed by television.

Implicit in the sex-role portrayals of much of television drama is the suggestion that marriage and parenthood are of greater significance in a woman's life than a man's life. Television's fictional world apparently places greater emphasis on establishing the marital status of its female characters. In an analysis of programme samples over a four-year period, Tedesco (1974) reported that marital status could be identified and coded for 51 percent of female characters, but for only 32 percent of male characters. At about the same time Downing (1974) reported another content analytic study which corroborated Tedesco's findings. Once again, marital status was (at least according to this particular researcher) portrayed as more crucial in the lives of women than of men in the world of television drama. Whether a character was married or single was identified more often for women (85 percent) than for men (73 percent).

A further point on this theme is the apparent confinement of women on television to a home life dominated by family and personal relationships and interests. Studies of dramatic television content have indicated that not only are female characters usually depicted in domestic settings but that they also seem to be much more concerned about family and personal matters than men, *outside* the home as well as in it. McNeil (1975), for example, showed that personal relationships associated with romance or family problems accounted for 74 percent of female interactions but only 18 percent of male interactions. On the other hand, professional or work-orientated interactions constituted only 15 percent of women's versus 35 percent of men's relationships on television drama programmes.

Additional support for the personal or familial orientation of women's relationships on television comes from the general finding that women are numerically better represented in soap operas and situation comedies whose settings are predominantly domestic. In soap operas, women appear in almost equal numbers with men and female characters are usually more central to the plot in these programmes than they are in action/ adventure programmes. In addition to their higher visibility, soap opera females often hold respected positions in the family and immediate social environment (Downing, 1974). But whilst, on the surface, this suggests greater balance in the depiction of women and men, many of the characteristics of the daytime serial females continue to reflect the conventional images of women found in action-drama content. Following a content analysis of 300 episodes from fifteen television serials, Downing (1974) revealed a persistence of sex-segregated role divisions in which women were concerned mostly with their physical appearance and marital relationships, while the world of work was still largely the preserve of males.

The major action in most soap operas and situation comedies consists of conversation, the nature of which centres on romance, familial and other interpersonal relationships, and problems with these relationships — once again reflecting the traditional female stereotypes (Katzman, 1972). Thus, in these programmes even when women are shown outside the home environment (e.g., at work), their conversations tend to revolve around domestic matters.

Sex-stereotyping of occupational roles in television drama in the United States was highlighted in several studies during the early 1970s. Although the actual percentage distribution of the sexes in work contexts on television varied from one study to another, the overall pattern was one of under-representation of female characters in employment relative to male characters *and* compared with the participation of women in the labour force in the real world. Downing (1974) reported that in the sample of prime-time television output she examined, 58 percent of men were shown in professional occupations against just 19 percent of women.

McNeil (1975) found that not only were women portrayed proportionately more often than men in marital roles, but also that the percentage of characters who were employed differed significantly according to sex. Almost 75 percent of the male television population were depicted as gainfully employed, while less than 50 per cent of female characters held jobs. Among married characters, the disparity was even greater. Few married women, and fewer mothers were portrayed as employed. Working wives and mothers generally appeared in comedy shows, where their work status was rarely elaborated. According to McNeil, in the few instances when television women held high-prestige positions, they played less important roles and their work activities were not central to the plot. Female characters generally worked under close supervision and had far less authority than men.

Sex-trait stereotyping. A prominent stereotype of women in our culture is that they are more emotional than men. The emotional woman is believed to become flustered in the most minor crisis; she is seen as sensitive, often fearful and anxious, and generally dependent on male help and support in all kinds of personal and professional situations. With respect to television, some writers have argued that portrayals convey an impression of the 'emotional' woman that is often inaccurate and unfair. Indeed in more general terms, it seems that there has been a significant sex-bias in the way behaviours have been labelled emotional (Sherman, 1971). Emotionality tends to refer most often to those reactions — fearfulness, anxiety, moodiness and neuroticism — which are typically associated with women, but less often to overt responses — aggression and dominance — which are regarded as masculine traits.

We have already seen that evidence from content analysis research has been interpreted predominantly to support the argument that television drama tends to confine women to the home and family where their lives are dominated by personal relationships. While men are frequently faced with problems related to the outside world and work, women are shown by television to be much more involved in family and romantic conflicts in which their 'characteristic' emotionality is highlighted (McNeil, 1975). Following an analysis of US peak-time television programme samples over three television seasons from 1975 to 1978, Greenberg, Richards and Henderson (1980) reported that women were portrayed as needing emotional support more often than men. Men, on the other hand, more often needed physical support of various kinds. Together, these findings indicated a generalised sex-stereotyping pattern in which male television characters were orientated more towards physical needs, while female characters were orientated towards emotional needs.

Is there evidence that females are in fact more emotional in these particular ways? The answer seems to depend on the type of measure of emotional responsiveness that is used. With regard to fearfulness, females have been found to be somewhat more emotional when rating scale measures are used (e.g., Spiegler and Liebert, 1970; Wilson, 1966, 1967), but observational studies of sex differences in response to a frightening stimulus in young children have not produced consistent results (Bronson, 1970; Maccoby and Jacklin, 1973; Stern and Bender, 1974). Overall though there does seem to be a general tendency for females to display more emotionality than males, at least after early childhood. But there is a further problem of interpretation, particularly of investigations of anxiety and fearfulness using paper-and-pencil tests. As males are socialised to hide their emotions, whereas females are expected openly to admit and display their feelings, it is therefore possible that sex-differences arise as a result of males being less willing to report their anxieties and fears than females (Frieze et al, 1978). In fact, a few studies have indicated support for this hypothesis (Spiegler and Liebert, 1970; Wilson, 1967). In these studies people who reported few fears or anxieties were also likely to score high on a measure of social desirability — the tendency to respond in culturally-approved ways. Much less ambiguity is present in the way women are characterised and portrayed on television however.

Another particularly important issue that is frequently highlighted by critics of the way television portrays the sexes is that relating to the dominance of men and the subordination of women. Analysis of the demographics of men and women and of behavioural sequences involving interactions between male and female characters have indicated that television could possibly cultivate the belief that men are naturally more competent and more powerful than women.

Focusing chiefly on demographic indicators of dominance, Lemon (1978) described an *intersex measure* — a method of analysis of sex-role portrayals on television drama which divided two-party interactions between men and women into those dominated by men, those dominated by women and those where men and women were portrayed as equals. A second and interrelated measure devised by the same author was called the *percentage of total appearances measure* which contrasted the number of times someone of a particular sex was portrayed as dominant, dominated, or equal with the total number of times members of that sex participated in such dyadic interactions.

Lemon found that one of the most important defining attributes of power and competence was occupational status. Men tended to be portrayed more often than women in high-prestige occupations — and they also gave more orders. However, even during interactions between the sexes where professional status was irrelevant, men still generally dominated women. There were variations in the pattern of domination-subordination between different programme genres. On her intersex measure, Lemon found that men dominated women in 23 percent of situation-comedy interactions, were dominated by women in 13 percent of interactions, and were portrayed as the equals of women in 65 percent of interactions. This pattern was more pronounced in crime-dramas, however, where men were dominant 47 percent of the time, were dominated six percent of the time and were equals with women the remaining 47 percent of the time.

One problem with this study which clouds the meaning of its findings is that Lemon was not clear on her definition of dominance in interpersonal interaction. Was the dominance of one character over another usually a function of the demographic (i.e., occupational or other social) position to which each was respectively allocated, or was it more often a function of the behavioural sequences which occurred between males and females and the outcomes of their behaviours for each of them?

Other researchers have been more precise in their definition of measurement of dominance between the sexes, sometimes analysing several different categories of behaviour to show differential patterns of power and competence among males and females in television drama. Among those behaviours analysed are order-giving and receiving, advice-giving and receiving; support-seeking and the ability to make plans and carry them through. Evidence on support-seeking has been discussed already under the emotionality of women on television, but male superiority is perhaps demonstrated even more clearly by patterns of order and advice giving and receiving among the sexes.

Turow (1974) studied patterns of advice-giving and receiving and order-giving and receiving between men and women in a sample of twelve hours of daytime programming and twelve hours of prime-time programming consisting mainly of soap operas and other dramatic television content. Turow reported that men gave orders or advice in 70 percent of all episodes of advice or order giving. Results of this analysis were interpreted to show that in the world of television drama, characters are apparently selected, occupations assigned and plots developed in such a way as to minimise the chances of women displaying superior knowledge or abilities to men. Furthermore, even when female characters were given such opportunities, the advice or order-giving tended to be concerned with traditionally female topics.

Manes and Melnyk (1974) carried out two studies in which they examined the models of female achievement available to television viewers. These studies surveyed television's portrayal both of achievement behaviour and its social consequences for the female achiever. The first study compared female models at four levels of achievement and showed that only those models at the lowest level of achievement were depicted as having successful social relations with men. The message thus offered is that women who are ambitious in a professional sense may have to forfeit a happy social and private life.

In their second study, Manes and Melnyk compared the marital status of male and female job holders on television. Compared with male job holders, females were depicted as less likely to be married, less likely to be successfully married, and more likely to be unsuccessfully or unhappily married. Content counts revealed that female characters who held jobs were ten times as likely to be unsuccessful in marriage as were housewives. The authors suggest, from their findings, that female achievers portrayed on television are depicted in a way that does not encourage female viewers to imitate their behaviour and in fact serves to inhibit achievement-oriented behaviour in female viewers. As with so many analyses of this sort, however, an assumption is made that the meanings read into television portrayals by the researchers are simililarly apprehended by the viewers. But this may not necessarily be true. Indeed, whilst television drama portrayals of women who are both successful in a career and happy in their home life may be less commonplace on the screen than portrayals in which success is achieved in only one sphere, the former may be more outstanding in the minds of viewers and provide more salient models for emulation.

Another example of the relative competence of the sexes on television is to be found in the extent to which male and female characters seem to be in control of events in their lives. One of the most extensively researched variables in the psychological literature on competence is 'attribution of causality'. According to this concept, people can be broadly categorised into those who believe they have a great deal of personal control over determining life's outcomes and those who believe that their lives are controlled primarily by forces external to themselves which they cannot influence. De Charms (1976) introduced the terms 'origin-like' (feeling of having personal control over events) and 'pawn-like' (feeling of not having personal control over events) to distinguish these two types of individual. Subsequently, Hodges, Brandt and Kline (1981) conducted a study in which they catalogued the frequencies with which male and female characters in peak-time family shows, violent-action shows, and daytime serials made statements which according to a scheme developed by de Charms could be classified either as 'origin-like' or 'pawn-like'

Hodges and colleagues found that in violent action shows and in family shows, female characters made substantially fewer origin statements than did males. Sex differences were especially pronounced in violent action shows where females made twice as many 'pawn-like' as 'origin-like' statements, while the pattern for males was of the same degree but in the opposite direction. According to the authors, from the perspective of social learning theory which would predict that viewers are likely to be influenced in their own behaviours by the behaviours of television characters similar to themselves, female viewers would be most likely to identify with and model themselves after female television actors. They argue therefore that the less favourable depiction of women than men in violent action shows for which at least half of US viewers are female, might lead to a lowering of female self-esteem. Unfortunately they provide no empirical evidence bearing directly on this hypothetical assumption. As we shall see in a later discussion of viewers' perceptions of the sexes, distinctions are often made between the world of television and the real world and it would be wrong to assume that viewers passively accept all that is presented to them on the screen.

Children's programmes

In so far as television may have a socialising influence on the beliefs, attitudes and behaviour of its audience, investigation of the content profiles of children's programmes and the sex-role concepts they may communicate to young viewers is of more than a little interest. A series of American content-analytic studies conducted during the early and mid-1970s indicated that children's programming on US network television tended to be more sexist than adult programming.

Early evidence for the lack of balance in sex-role portrayals on American television came from Levinson (1973) who reported that male characters outnumbered female characters by three to one in Saturday morning children's cartoons on the three major US networks. Even three out of four of the animal characters were identified as males. In another study of US network children's programmes, O'Kelly (1974) found that males heavily outnumbered females by 85 percent to 15 percent, and that adult male characters appeared more frequently on the screen than did adult females. Males also enjoyed a much broader range of occupations than females, with females most often portrayed in marital or familial roles. This last finding was repeated in other studies of children's programmes during this period. Cantor (1973) observed that male characters were more likely to have occupations than female characters in these programmes. Busby (1975) meanwhile found that women were depicted in only a narrow range of occupations.

The physical portrayal of women observed in children's programmes, as indicated elsewhere in television by American researchers, emphasised youth and attractiveness. Women on television, whether single or married, were invariably slim and attractive. Not only did female characters appear as very attractive, they were also portrayed as very concerned with the way they looked (Long and Simon, 1974).

The other great concerns of the women portrayed in children's programmes were their homes and their families. Female characters were more likely to be married than were male characters, but even though more prevalent in the marital context, they were not dominant in it. The status of married women observed in children's and family shows assessed by Long and Simon (1974) was one of deference to and dependency on their husbands. Women were no more likely to be portrayed in authority at home than at work. This was so even though, as observed elsewhere, married women tended to be attractive and youthful whilst their partners tended quite often to have gone to seed physically (Busby, 1974). The conclusion consistently reached by content-analytic researchers during the early seventies was that television represents women and men in a highly stereotyped manner, and if it influences children's sex-role perceptions at all it probably reinforces the status quo.

Further American studies of children's programmes conducted throughout the latter half of the 1970s and into the early 1980s revealed few changes in the way women were portrayed. An analysis of 20 hours of Saturday morning children's programming on the US networks by Nolan, Galst and White (1977) indicated that males still outnumbered females by three to one. Subsequently, Barcus (1978) analysed 899 characters from weekday and weekend children's programmes and found the same ratio of male characters to female characters. At weekends, the margin of difference was four to one in favour of males. This imbalance was found to be characteristic of all types of fictional and entertainment programming. More recently, Barcus (1983) replicated the above ratios following an analysis of an even larger sample of over 1100 television characters from children's programmes.

In another study Sternglanz and Serbin (1974) directed their attention to the consequences of a wide range of behaviours involving male-female interactions in cartoon programmes. The outcomes of male-instigated and female-instigated actions differed significantly: males were more often treated with positive (or rewarding) outcomes for their actions, whilst females tended to experience neutral or negative outcomes. Elaborating on this finding Sternglanz and Serbin suggested that children would be 'taught' different lessons by these portrayals according to whether they identified with male or female characters. The behavioural sequences analysed from these cartoons involved making and carrying out plans. Young girls who identified with female characters, who were generally unsuccessful in their achievements, would be shown that it is inappropriate for a woman to make plans and carry them out because more likely than not she will be punished for doing so.

Later studies of children's programme content have continued to record sex-role stereotyping in the way women and men are portrayed. In particular, in the context of occupations and careers, men continue, so it seems, to enjoy more variety and greater success at work. Schechtman (1978) assessed the distribution of male versus female occupational portrayals in terms of occupational prestige on six television shows which had been most frequently mentioned by preschool children as ones they watched — *Batman, Bugs Bunny, The Flintstones, Happy Days, Road Runner* and *Sesame Street*. Schechtman divided occupations into four ranges of occupational prestige — high, medium, low and very low — and explored patterns of distribution of occupational portrayals. From this analysis, he concluded that television, as a source of incidental learning about the world of work, offers the child a male-dominated picture of the occupational world. Women were generally portrayed in inferior occupational roles and in proportions not representing real world numbers. Men outnumbered women in all occupational prestige categories. No women at all are portrayed in the high level occupational prestige category.

Schechtman did not restrict his research purely to an analysis of television content however. He went on to assess possible relationships between television portrayals and the career awareness of pre-school children. He found that 95 per cent of the children he questioned named an occupational choice for adulthood. Furthermore, there was a strong relationship between the occupational choice prestige levels of boys and girls and the occupational prestige level of their favourite television character's occupation.

Advertisements directed at adults

In 1972 the New York Times Magazine published the first major content study of television commercials conducted by the National Organisation for Women (NOW). Over 1200 television commercials were content analysed over a period of one-and-a-half years by 100 NOW supporters in New York city (Hennessee and Nicholson, 1972). Over one-third of the advertisements monitored, claimed the authors, showed women as the domestic agents of men and as dependent on men. Nearly one-fifth showed women as sex objects and a similar proportion showed them as unintelligent. Over four out of ten commercials portrayed women as household functionaries. Often, women turned up in advertisements for food or cleaning products. NOW monitors also noted that women never seemed to tell men what to do; in television commercials men were constantly advising women.

Published for a general readership, exact details of the NOW methodology were not given, but it seems on the basis of the information that was supplied that the study may have been unreliable. There is some uncertainty surrounding the professionnalism of the monitoring techniques employed, and some doubt must be cast on the homogeneity of the large number of coders in the ways they classified women in advertisements along subjective judgemental dimensions such as 'submissive', 'intelligent' and 'dependent'.

The first major academic study of female stereotyping in television commercials was conducted at around the same time.

19

Dominick and Rauch (1972) sampled almost 1,000 television advertisements, again from network stations in New York City, during April, 1971. These researchers coded commercials for, among other things, the products being advertised, sex of voice-over, sex of prime purchaser, the role played by the woman in the advertisement, and the apparent occupation of the female presented. The appearance of men in a selection of commercials was also monitored for comparisons between the sexes.

Once again, a pronounced pattern of sex-stereotyping was reported, with 75 percent of all advertisements using females being for products generally found at home in the kitchen or bathroom.

According to the authors, the television commercials they studied conveyed the message that a woman's place is in the home; 38 percent of women in the sampled commercial population were shown inside the home versus only 14 percent of men. The single largest occupation for females was housewife with over half so portrayed. Men were generally more often in authority roles within commercials. When women were shown outside the home in some sort of occupation, they were more often than not in a job subservient to men. Voice-overs were predominantly male; 87 percent of coded commercials used a male voice, six percent a female one and seven percent a chorus. In addition, 60 percent of the on-camera product representatives shown were male.

A couple of years later, Courtney and Whipple (1974) provided a longitudinal and comparative analysis of the portrayal of women in television advertisements drawing on four studies conducted over a two-year spell between April 1971 and February 1973. Included in their analysis were the findings of the NOW and Dominick and Rauch studies. Their major conclusions reinforced the earlier findings. Women were shown mainly as housewives and mothers, while men were shown in at least twice as many occupations. Almost 40 percent of women were shown in domestic settings at home compared to about 15 percent of men. Female product representatives were shown most often performing domestic duties, while males may have demonstrated product features but did not actually use the products. Men were responsible for the vast majority of voice-overs (85 percent) and dominated as on-camera product representatives on prime-time television advertisements. Over the two years of the study, Courtney and Whipple noted, however, that the number of female product representatives did increase significantly, particularly on daytime television where they appeared as often as male representatives.

At around the same time, another study of the sexes in US television commercials was undertaken by McArthur and Resko (1975). While their principal findings reflect those of Dominick and Rauch, the interest in this study lies in its examination of authority roles in advertisements. Seventy percent of men were presented as authorities, but only 30 percent by virtue of product use. Of the 14 percent of women who were product authorities, 86 percent were portrayed as product users. Men were also much more likely than women to give an argument for the use of products.

Similar findings to the above with respect to the occupational roles, voice-overs, product representation and product category associations of women in television advertisements were reported by Silverstein and Silverstein (1975). These researchers also found that although women sometimes gave advice in commercials for female and household products, men gave advice more often in every product category.

Throughout the mid-1970s, further American studies continued to find pronounced stereotyping in the way women were portrayed in television commercials. Focusing yet again on the relative portrayed expertise of males and females, Maracek, Piliavin and others (1978) reported a more even distribution of voice-over experts between the sexes across three years of monitoring (1972, 1973 and 1974). However, female voice-overs were associated with a fairly limited range of product categories — food, household, or feminine care products. Within these traditionally female product categories there was a marked increase in the extent to which the female was the last word of authority heard.

During the second half of the decade, further studies indicated that while males and females appeared in equal numbers as product representatives, women still were predominantly found in commercials for domestic products and invariably appeared in the home. Men, on the other hand, dominated the non-domestic product categories and settings. The male also continued to be the voice of authority (O'Donnell and O'Donnell, 1978).

Later studies have noted a few slight and subtle changes in the portrayal of the sexes in television advertisements, though the old patterns of stereotyping still largely prevail. Schneider (1979) reported trends in sex-role portrayals on television commercials from 1971 to 1976. They monitored a sample of approximately 300 commercials aired in Minneapolis-St Paul during October 1976 which they compared to Dominick and Rauch's (1971) sample. Over this time they observed certain changes in the patterns of sex-role portrayals, but also that stereotyping was still prevalent. There were differences in the demographic profile of television advertisements monitored by Schneider and those analysed by Dominick and Rauch. More older people were shown in the 1976 commercial sample, though there was still more emphasis on youth among women than among men. Married men and women were both under-represented in 1976 television advertisements compared to census population figures, but women were more often portrayed as married than men by 20 percent. It was also found that fewer members of both sexes were portrayed as employed in 1976 compared with 1971, but the gap between men and women had narrowed. Although women were no more or less likely to be in out-of-home settings, more men were shown in the home in the latter half of the 1970s.

Knill, Pesch, Pursey, Gilpin and Perloff (1981) reported a content analysis of over 1600 commercials aired on daytime and prime-time US network television, and examined changes in sex role portrayals since the mid-1970s. On daytime television, over 90 per cent of voice-overs were supplied by males. Female product representatives far outnumbered males in afternoon television commercials, but there was a distinct variation in the occupational settings of female and male characters. Over 80 percent of female product representatives were shown in family or home occupations, while nearly 70 percent of male product representatives were portrayed in business or management occupations.

During prime-time, 90 percent of voice-overs were male, dominating all product types. Males and females were equally likely to be seen as product representatives in prime time, but the majority of women were still shown in the home and the majority of men in business settings. Knill et al concluded that during the 1970's television commercials persisted with images predominantly of the 'traditional' women, though the margin of difference between professional women and professional men shown in advertisements was decreasing.

Using a coding frame modelled very closely on that developed by American researchers McArthur and Resko (1975), Manstead and McCulloch (1981) conducted a study to examine the portrayal of men and women in a sample of British television advertisements. They analysed 170 commercials from peak-time television in the north-west ITV region in Britain over one week. The analysis revealed that men and women were portrayed in markedly different ways.

Women were more likely than men to be shown as product users. Women were shown more often than men in the home. Women were apparently displayed in dependent roles more often than men were. Finally, women provided no arguments in favour of the advertised products with which they appeared. In other words, the nature of the differences in sex-role portrayals was systematic and in accordance with traditional sex roles. Men were typically portrayed as having expertise and authority, as being objective and knowledgeable about reasons for buying particular products, as occupying roles which are autonomous, and as being concerned with the practical consequences of product purchase.

Manstead and McCulloch noted many similarities in the way the sexes were portrayed in commercials in Britain and America and one major difference in the way the use of arguments was portrayed among central figures. McArthur and Resko reported that 30 percent of their female central figures used no argument at all, whereas Manstead and McCulloch found that 63 percent of central female figures used no product argument.

Another difference concerned the relation between the sex of the central figure and the types of rewards associated with particular products. McArthur and Resko found no reliable correlation between the sex of product users and the rewards suggested by these consumers, whereas Manstead and McCulloch found that females were significantly more likely than males to be shown suggesting social approval and self-enhancement rewards, rather than practical or other rewards. These British researchers concluded that on balance the portrayal of adults was more sex-role stereotyped in British than in American commercials.

Manstead and McCulloch's study was replicated in part by Chappell (1983), but he coded neither the types of arguments used to endorse products nor the types of products advertised.

More recently, two more British studies of television advertising content have emerged, elaborating slightly on the coding frame used by Manstead and McCulloch. Livingstone and Green (1986) coded sex-role portrayals in 175 evening advertisements recorded over a seven-day period from one ITV region. Harris and Stobart (1986) examined 138 advertisements broadcast in another ITV over a 12-day period during both the afternoon and evening. Both studies reinforced earlier findings that television advertisements in Britain tend to portray men and women in disparate and essentially traditional stereotyped ways.

Male characters were much more likely than female characters to be shown as product authorities in autonomous roles (e.g. professional, celebrity, interviewer) who offered arguments, often factual, in favour of the product, which was usually non-domestic. Female characters were considerably more likely than males to be shown as product consumers in family, domestic settings, associated with personal, household and food products.

Livingstone and Green also found that men were more likely than women to advertise expensive products and to provide voice-overs. Women were more likely to be visually presented and to remain silent while men spoke in favour of products. In considering the value of products, it emerged that expensive products were associated with the most masculine men and the most feminine women were silent. An extra feature considered by Harris and Stobart was time of day. Female figures were more prominent in daytime advertisements and offered more factual arguments in favour of products. In the evening, however, males were in the majority as central figures providing product endorsements.

Some mention should also be made briefly of a further British study which analysed radio advertisements (Furnham and Schofield, 1986). No sex differences were found for presentation of arguments, product reward, product type, and accent of character. More women than men, however, were presented in domestic locations. On the whole, radio advertisements were not found to be as sex-stereotyped as those on television.

Advertisements directed at children

There is a small number of published US studies concerning sex-role portrayals in television advertisements directed at children. As with advertisements directed at adult audiences, advertisements on children's television have been found to contain a preponderance of male characters.

Two American studies during the early 1970s found that this was certainly true of advertisements broadcast during Saturday morning's children's programmes. Winick, Williamson, Chuzmir and Winick (1973) found that 58 percent of children's advertisements contained boys, while only 36 percent included females. Thirty-five percent contained males only, 19 percent females only, and the rest featured both sexes. Chulay and Francis also found that girls in children's advertisements were most likely to be shown in ads for food, games, and dolls, while boys were mainly in ads for games, toy cars and toy planes. Boys were also more likely to be shown playing outdoors, while girls more usually played inside the home. The imaginary roles girls and boys took on in the games they played were also identified as highly stereotyped. Girls often played house-wife or mother figures, while boys were soldiers, pilots or racing drivers. The authors suggest that children's ads present girls only in traditional stereotyped roles, and that this might lead to a narrowing of ideas about women amongst youngsters especially with respect to their being successful in the business world.

McArthur and Eisen (1976), analysed 161 advertisements broadcast during children's programmes on US television. Of the central characters in these advertisements, 80 percent were male and 20 percent were female. The imbalance of males to females found here was much more marked than that reported by McArthur and Resko (1975) for adult-oriented advertisements. These results were supported by a study of televised toy advertisements during the 1977 and 1978 Christmas holiday season in the US (Feldstein and Feldstein, 1982). Not only were there more male-oriented than female-oriented advertisements, but on average there were also more boys than girls per advertisement.

Summary

In summary, descriptive studies of the content of adults' and children's programmes and advertisements have revealed a persistent sexism in the portrayal of women and men on television. Not only are women grossly outnumbered by men, but the range of roles women play is more limited. From these descriptive accounts of television's sex-role portrayals, some researchers have been tempted to draw certain conclusions about the cultivation of sex-sterotyped conceptions through regular television viewing, especially among malleable children during their early developmental years. This kind of inference, however, assumes that the meanings identified by descriptive analyses of television portrayals are the same as those perceived by viewers. Since content analysis does not assess audience perceptions of or reactions to television programmes or advertisements, however, there is no way of telling from this kind of research alone if viewers 'see' the same sorts of things on the screen as do researchers. According to some researchers, television programming tends to be stereotyped in its presentation of the sexes. But it could be that portrayals that go against the grain, although less commonly occurring, are the ones which stand out for viewers at a perceptual level.

Chapter 3

Perceptions of the sexes

Research into the way the sexes are depicted on television has indicated that portrayals of women and men are stereotyped and repetitive, and according to some writers, lag far behind the social changes that are taking place in the world today (Butler and Paisley, 1980). It is often assumed that this stereotyping of both the roles and traits of the sexes on the screen engenders a parallel pattern of beliefs about the sexes among those who regularly watch television.

Some writers have envisaged a process of influence in which greater amounts of television viewing can produce biased or distorted beliefs about the world that are consistent with television's stereotyped portrayals (see Gerbner and Gross, 1976; Gerbner et al, 1977). It is assumed that mass audiences assimilate information, often incidentally, from television programmes, which may influence the way they think about the world around them. Continuous exposure to television may cultivate public beliefs about various social entities that are consonant with images of these entities portrayed on television. Thus, stereotyped television portrayals (and the 'messages' they convey) concerning sex roles may give rise to stereotyped beliefs about men and women especially among heavy viewers and those individuals whose beliefs on these matters are at an early stage of development (i.e., children). As we saw in the introduction to this monograph, sex-role development and the adaptation of sex-appropriate attitudes and behaviours occur early in children's lives and media content may provide raw material on which youngsters formulate their ideas about the sexes.

A number of different views on the socialisation of sex-roles have emerged from prominent developmental theorists that have opened up the possibility of television having cultivation effects on children's sex-role development by positioning theoretical accounts of sex-role learning without any direct interaction between teacher and learner. One influential cognitive-developmental view is that children learn during the first few years of life that their gender is unchangeable and are therefore motivated to value highly those attributes and behaviours culturally expected of their own sex in order to maintain self-esteem (Kohlberg, 1966). An alternative, social-learning view has asserted that children are rewarded for imitating members of their own sex and therefore attend more closely to and learn more from same-sex models (Grusec and Brinker, 1972; Mischel, 1970).

Although now an apparently theoretically feasible proposition, it is difficult in practice to isolate the relative contribution of the media to children's sex-role development. Television viewing, for instance, is so commonplace, even among pre-school children, that it is difficult to find an adequate control group which have not been exposed to this media content. As television *viewing*, rather than *non-viewing*, is the norm these days, any group of non-viewers is likely to be unusual in many important respects apart from media usage and these factors might account wholly or at least in part for differences between their sex-role perceptions and those of regular television users. To get round this problem, some investigators have tested a weaker hypothesis which states that the more one watches stereotyped television content, the more likely it is that one will be affected by it in terms of stereotyped opinions or behaviours. These 'cultivation effects' are measured by comparing the beliefs of heavy and light television viewers to indicate associations between particular types of opinion and levels of television watching. Unfortunately, this model embodies many problematical assumptions about causal relationships between what is shown on television and the formation of particular perceptions, belief and opinions among viewers about the world in which they live. One assumption is that 'messages' inferred from programme content profiles concerning various social groups are recognised and encoded by audiences, who assimilate them into their existing knowledge structures. It is also assumed that heavy viewers will be more strongly influenced by television's messages than will light viewers purely as a function of greater volume of exposure to them. However, measures of *amount* of viewing may not be valid and sufficient indicators of television effects, because television content and viewers' preferences for that content vary considerably, and two heavy viewers who watch totally different kinds of programmes may hold two quite disparate sets of beliefs as a result. Relatively little research has been done on how people perceive television's images of women. Content analyses, from which inferences about television-effects are often made, may actually be poor indicators of audience perceptions (Ceulemans and Fauconnier, 1979; Perloff, Brown and Miller, 1982). As we shall see in the sections to follow, even where direct tests of social attitudes towards women have been employed, researchers (with a few exceptions) have usually not related these reactions to specific viewing habits and preferences of individuals.

We need to know not simply *how much* television individuals watch but also *what kinds of content* they prefer to watch most often. Which particular portrayals are most salient to viewers and most likely to hold their attention? And finally, to what extent are the messages conveyed by television portrayals assimilated by viewers into their existing knowledge structures? If it is true that boys and girls learn to value most those attributes and those activities which are presented by society as appropriate for their own sex, then it follows that they may also be likely to pay close attention to and show strong preference for television portrayals featuring same-sex characters.

People learn to ascribe certain personality attributes as well as behaviours to men or to women. For example, some writers have pointed out that traits such as nurturance, dependence and passivity are typically classified as feminine, while dominance and aggression are generally considered as masculine (Bem, 1974; Rosenkrantz, Vogel, Bec, Broverman and Broverman, 1968).

Furthermore, analyses of television content profiles have indicated that television portrayals tend to emphasise certain of these sex-typed characteristics in men and women (Paisley and Butler, 1980; Tuchman et al, 1978). What evidence is there though that traits emphasized on television are also the ones most salient to viewers? We shall now turn our attention to what is known about audience members' perceptions of the way women and men are depicted on television. We shall first look at evidence concerning children's perceptions of the sexes on television before turning to examine recent evidence on adults' perceptions.

Children's perceptions of the sexes on TV

There is some evidence that children prefer television characters of their own sex. Maccoby and Wilson (1957) observed this tendency early on with respect to movie characters. They asked 12-year-old girls and boys to name their favourite character in a movie, to say which part they would themselves most like to play, and the character they would most like to be. Ninety percent of the girls and 84 percent of the boys answered the majority of these questions with the same-sex character from the film.

Sex-biased preferences have been found among even younger children. Joy, Kimball and Zabrock (1977) showed five and six-year-olds a short videotaped drama featuring two adult characters. Afterwards, the children were asked a series of questions including which character they liked better — Mary or John? Of the boys, 71 percent chose John, and 85 percent of the girls chose Mary.

In addition to self-reported preferences, children may selectively attend to same-sex characters on television and interpret sex-role images or themes in programmes according to what they already know about sex roles. One researcher has found that when four to nine-year-old children were questioned about sex-stereotyped television material, they exhibited a ready ability to elaborate upon scenes in ways dependent on existing understanding about sex-roles (Durkin, 1984). Children could explain, for example, that hypothetical fathers, not actually seen in a programme, were "out at work", while mothers not seen were "washing the dishes". These youngsters were able to account for a range of male and female television portrayals in this way.

Mayes and Valentine (1979) found that young viewers tended to perceive sex-typed attributes in television cartoon characters. Whilst this study did not demonstrate cultivation effects, it does indicate that cartoon characters, who may just conceivably provide role models for children, were seen to exhibit stereotypical sex-role behaviours and attributes. In this experiment, however, viewers were primed to focus on certain aspects of programme content, a feature which is not typical of ordinary viewing. To what extent do young viewers pay different amounts of attention to the presence and nature of male and female television characters when they are not given specific instructions to do so before watching a programme?

Evidence on this has emerged from a study by Sprafkin and Liebert (1976) who examined how boys and girls select and attend to male- and female-dominated scenes on television. Groups of youngsters were shown film sequences which featured female characters displaying female-appropriate behaviour, or male characters displaying male-appropriate behaviour, or males and/or females engaged in relatively less rigid sex-role portrayals. While boys selected and attended to male-focused programmes more than to female-focused programmes and attended specifically to male-dominated scenes in those programmes, precisely the opposite was true of girls who were more likely to prefer programmes or scenes that revolved around female characters and activities. Girls were no more likely to attend to male-focused programmes or scenes than were boys to attend to female-focused materials. Also boys and girls identified to the same extent with same-sex characters, and same-sex characters were named as favourites by 84 percent of children.

More recent research, however, has indicated that male characters on the screen may often attract greater attention from young viewers of both sexes than do female characters, and that evaluations of female characters may be especially harsh and recall of what they do or say particularly poor among female members of the audience. In a non-television study, McArthur

31

and Eisen (1976) found that preschool boys persisted longer on a task after hearing a story about achievement by a male character than a story about a female character, although no significant trend in the opposite direction was observed for girls.

In a subsequent study that investigated differences in children's learning from male and female television newscasters, Tan, Raudy, Huff and Miles (1980) found interesting interactions between the sex of the viewer and sex of the newscaster in relation to perceived credibility and retention of the news. Groups of eight to eleven year-old children viewed one of two specially prepared 15 minute newscasts, one of which was read by a female newscaster and the other by a male newscaster. Results showed that the male newsreader was generally more effective than the female newsreader in producing retention of newscast material, and that boys remembered more of the newscast than did girls. Although children rated newsreaders of both sexes equally believable, in a test of news recall, girls remembered significantly less from the female newsreader. Tan et al suggest that their results may indicate something about the way boys and girls appraised male and female newscasters. While boys may have considered the role of TV newscasting to be appropriate for both men and women, girls may not have perceived this particular role as appropriate for their own sex. Girls may therefore have paid less attention to the news when it was read by a female newscaster.

Further evidence has emerged that pre-existing sex-stereotypes among young viewers may distort their perceptions and memories for television portrayals. Drabman, Robertson, Patterson, Jarvie, Hammer, and Cordua (1982) showed pre-school and elementary school children a videotape of a male nurse and female doctor. Afterwards, the children were asked to identify photographs or names of the doctor and nurse. Reversing what they actually saw, most children up the age of 12 years, tended to select male pictures and names for the doctor and female pictures and names for the nurse. Only the oldest children (age 12 years) correctly identified the names of the doctor and nurse.

These findings have received further support from work done in the United States by Williams, La Rose and Frost (1981) and in the United Kingdom by Durkin (1983). Williams et al investigated the impact of a television series aimed at teaching counter-stereotyping. In one experiment they showed four segments from the prospective series to groups of children. These segments portrayed male and female characters enacting some typical role for their particular sex. The principal male character in the series was a well known actor who had formerly appeared in M*A*S*H*, and was shown as a man who could mix strength and leadership with gentleness and supportiveness. Another teenage female character was shown as someone who not only possessed the usual feminine qualities but also was a person who could assume leadership and take risks in ways normally associated only with males.

Teenage boys and girls were shown these programme segments and afterwards were asked questions about how much they liked what they had seen, how much they understood what was shown and how inclined they were to emulate aspects of a particular character's behaviour. It was found that different children like and perceive different things in counter-stereotyped television portrayals.

Opinions about what they saw varied both as a function of the sex of the child and in relation to the sex of the television character in question. Boys' evaluations of male and female characters from the television series indicated that the more they saw a male character in a stereotyped way, the more they liked him, whereas the more counter-stereotyped a female character was perceived to be, the more boys liked her. The children had relatively strong factual comprehension of the television programmes, but their comprehension of the sex-role objectives of the programmes was lower than hoped for. Similarly, the desire to imitate the counter-stereotyped characters' behaviours were mixed and in some respects inconclusive.

Williams et al found overall a selective bias in perception of the programme materials, such that stereotypic males and non-stereotypic females seemed to be better liked and better remembered. This suggests that children may pay greater attention to masculine type behaviours, whether performed by male or female characters on the screen. On the other hand, attention to male characters behaving in a non-stereotypic fashion apparently is much weaker and may be the most difficult example of behaviour of all to get across.

In recent British research on young viewers' perceptions of counter-stereotypic role portrayals on television, Durkin (1983) investigated teenage girls' opinions about women in traditionally male roles. He conducted an experiment in which 79 pupils from a secondary school were selected to watch one of two versions of a television weather bulletin delivered by a woman forecaster. In one version, a male newsreader in the preceding news programme remarked favourably on the forecaster's new hairstyle, while in another version, this remark was edited out. The children were shown the forecast and then answered a number of questions about the forecaster herself (her qualifications, looks, dress, presentation style, experience and reliability), and about whether they would like to become a weather forecaster or newsreader themselves. The principal research question was what effect on childrens' opinions would the remark by the newsreader have.

Contrary to expectations, girls tended to see the forecaster as better qualified and more experienced in the version with the remark. Girls in both groups estimated the forecaster's experience as greater than boys did. This, suggests Durkin, may indicate that girls believe that women have to try harder. Girls also estimated the forecaster's qualifications to be slightly higher on average than did boys. Boys saw the forecaster as slightly more experienced and qualified in the edited version. This may indicate that the flattering (though some might say 'sexist') remark made by the male newsreader reduced the level of professionalism perceived by boys.

Adults' Perceptions of the Sexes on TV

Research on adults' perceptions of the sexes on television has investigated awareness of the relative presence of males and females on the screen and subjective ratings of the personality traits of males and females in television programmes and advertisements. These studies have sometimes revealed that viewers' subjective perceptions of the characteristics of males and females on television do not always correspond with the personality profiles of the sexes inferred in traditional content analytic research.

In analysing adult perceptions of Saturday morning cartoons on television, Sternglanz and Serbin (1974) showed ten different videotaped cartoon shows to college undergraduates who provided subjective ratings about male and female characters in them. These viewers reported that more male than female characters appeared in the cartoons; that females were usually shown in traditional occupational roles for women; and that female characters also tended to be characterised predominantly by typically 'feminine' personal attributes (ie, passivity, nurturance, submissiveness, dependence), whereas males were characterised by opposing 'masculine' attributes.

Scheibe (1979) had fourteen male and female viewers rate a sample forty-eight television commercials originally shown on-air in 1976. Judges rated the commercials using adjectival scales designed to measure the personality characteristics of the men and women portrayed. Some confirmation of earlier content analyses emerged from Scheibe's findings. Female characters in the commercials were perceived, for example, as more concerned about the appearance of their home and as more dependent on the opposite sex than were male characters. What is particularly interesting about Scheibe's findings, however, is the differences in perceptions of characters appearing in prime-time and daytime commercials. In general, female characters were perceived as less able spouses, less mature, more foolish, and less successful than male characters, but in daytime commercials the situation reversed and women were seen in a more positive light than men along similar dimensions. Scheibe concluded that, with respect to personality traits, male characters are portrayed as negatively as are female characters. The real difference comes with the time of day when the commercial is shown.

Sharits and Lammers (1982) extended Schneider's findings about perceptions of male and female personalities in television commercials. Using a similar methodology, male and female business school students were asked to rate their perceptions of the roles portrayed in over 100 television advertisements. Results showed that females in the commercials were rated more favourably than men in terms of many attributes. Females were perceived to be portrayed as better spouses and parents, more mature, more attractive, more interesting and more modern than males. Little difference was found in the perceptions of male and female judges. One final interesting observation made by Sharits and Lammers was that men seem to be increasingly filling sex-object roles in television advertisements.

In a study of the perceived personality traits of male and female characters in dramatic television programmes, Peevers (1979) recruited six judges to evaluate the principal males and females in selected television dramas using Bem's Sex Role Inventory. Bem's work on psychological androgyny (1974, 1975, 1976) has presented an alternative to traditional sex-role stereotypes. Instead of conceiving of an individual as primarily masculine or feminine, as though these characteristics existed along a single continuum, the concept of androgyny allows consideration of an individual in terms of the degree to which she/he possesses both kinds of qualities. To Bem, the androgynous person is mentally healthy, able to act competently in situations which require traditional male characteristics, and also in those in which stereotypical female characteristics are adaptive. In her 1974 study, for example, Bem found that androgynous males and females, as measured by the Bem Sex Role Inventory (BSRI) (Bem, 1974), showed more independence from social pressure to conform than did participants categorised as feminine. At the same time, traditionally feminine, playful and nurturant behaviour, was displayed to a significantly greater degree by androgynous and feminine males than by masculine males.

Peevers reported two studies conducted one year apart. In the first of these, results indicated that 85 percent of all male characters were classified in highly masculine terms, while only 44 percent of all ratings for females fell in the feminine range. In addition, 28 percent of female characters' sex-role scores were in the masculine range, compared with only four percent of male characters who had opposite sex scores. More than twice as many female characters scored in the androgynous range as did male characters (28 percent versus 11 percent). The second study replicated the first and indicated that males were perceived as being more stereotypical than females, thus presenting a contrast to the generally held notion that it is females who are highly and consistently stereotyped by the media.

Peevers' study indicated that the traditional male role is highly valued: so valued that it is over dramatised in TV programmes. The sex-role scores of many male characters were so extremely masculine that they could hardly be achieved by real people. The 'supermasculine', non-human portrayal of the male role abounded on the TV screen, presenting a continuing picture of an unattainable but supposedly desirable role model.

Analysis of the female role portrayal, on the other hand, revealed that it was more diversified, more flexible, and more human, in the sense that female characters' sex-role scores fell within the limits attainable by real people. According to Peevers, these results dramatically illustrated the acceptance of greater flexibility in the female role in our society. Deviations by female characters in the direction of masculine qualities were acceptable because those qualities are valued. Conversely, male deviations from the male role remained highly unacceptable.

Viewers' perceptions of the sex-role or sex-traits of television characters, however, may depend upon the way they perceive themselves. Goff, Goff and Lehrer (1980) explored young adults' perceptions of the qualities of five well-known female characters on US television using the Bem Sex-Role Inventory and also looked at how these perceptions were related to viewers' self-ratings on the same scale. Self-perceptions turned out to have stronger associations with character perceptions than did the actual sex of respondents.

Androgynous respondents were likely to perceive television characters in androgynous terms too. Respondents who saw themselves in masculine terms, however, perceived the characters to be more feminine; while more feminine-rated respondents perceived the characters in more masculine terms. These results provide evidence that the non sex-typed (androgynous) viewer is more perceptive of the blend of masculine and feminine personality characteristics portrayed by characters perhaps because his or her own personality is perceived to consist of a similar blend.

Despite the accusations which have derived from traditional content analysis studies that television is responsible for gross sex-sterotyping, the open-ended opinions of viewers have revealed a more complex pattern of images of women as seen on television. One recent survey which sought from viewers, their unprompted perceptions of the televised images of women found a diversity of responses among both male and female members of the audience (Atwood, Zahn and Webber, 1986).

Interviewees were asked to specify a recent instance in which they had seen a woman portrayed on television in a positive way, and to cite up to three reasons for evaluating the portrayal as positive. The same procedure was then repeated for any negative portrayals that had been seen.

Three-quarters of responses categorising women on television in a positive light did so because the portrayals were seen as showing women as strong, intelligent, professional and realistic. Just one-quarter of positive portrayals were attributes such as physical attractiveness, being nurturant or caring towards others. Viewers were much more likely to describe television portrayals of women as negative because the women were shown as weak, exploited victims, housewives, or sex objects. Having assertive, aggressive or selfish traits however was much less often likely to result in a negative evaluation of television women.

Perceptions of the sexes on TV and in everyday life. Recent British research has attempted to shed more light not only on how the sexes are seen by viewers on television, but also how these television perceptions differ from the way in which the sexes are seen in everyday life. During two weeks of programme appreciation measurement as routinely conducted by the IBA's Research Department, viewing diaries together with questionnaires were sent to representative samples in the Yorkshire and Central Scotland Independent Television regions of the United Kingdom*. The diaries listed all programmes broadcast on the four main UK television channels during each

---

*Viewing diaries and questionnaires were placed by interviewers with 640 people representative of the Yorkshire ITV region and with 640 people representative of the Central Scotland ITV region during one week spells of programme appreciation measurement in February and September 1984. Completed diaries together with questionnaires were returned by 505 people in Yorkshire, a return rate of 79 percent. Demographically, 49 percent of this return sample were males and 51 percent were females; broken down by age, 39 percent were 16-34 years, 32 percent were 35-54 years, and 29 percent were 55+ years; and in terms of socio-economic class, 29 percent

week. Respondents gave appreciation scores for all programmes seen, thus providing a record of their viewing for the week. The questionnaire listed ten propositions about women and then precisely equivalent propositions about men, and asked respondents to say how often each proposition was true of men or of women 'as they appear on television'. On the reverse side of the sheet the same propositions were presented and respondents were asked to repeat the exercise, but for men and women 'as they actually are in real life'. The propositions were designed to reflect traits identified by previous content analysis research as typical features of female and male portrayals on television (see Gunter, 1984; Towler, 1984).

Striking differences emerged between perceptions of men and women both on television and in real life. There were some variations as well between male and female respondents in the way women and men perceived either on television or in real life, indicating that viewers do make subtle distinctions between the TV images of the sexes and real world appearances and characteristics. These results are set out in Tables 1 and 2. Characteristics have been listed in a normative ranking in such a way that the ones at the top of the list are those which respondents consider characterise women in real life more than men ('womanly' attributes), and work down to the bottom of the list where people apparently feel that these attributes are more characteristic of men than of women in real life ('manly' attributes).

Overall, there was not much difference between men and women respondents in the extent to which either thought that 'womanly' attributes applied to women in real life or on television. Likewise the extent to which these five more 'womanly' attributes were noticed in men, varied but little overall between real life and television. There were, however, notewor-

---

were professional, middle class, 36 percent were skilled working class, and 35 percent were semi- and unskilled working class people. In Central Scotland, 494 people returned completed diaries together with questionnaires, a return rate of 77 percent. Demographically, 48 percent were males, and 52 percent were females; 44 percent were 16-36 years, 29 percent were 35-54 years, and 27 percent were 55+ years; 34 percent were professional, middle class, 31 percent were skilled working class, and 34 percent were semi- and unskilled working class people.

Table 1. *Percentages of female and male respondents who perceived each characteristic as true of women and men in real life and on TV.*

Those evaluated:	REAL LIFE				TELEVISION			
	Women		Men		Women		Men	
Perceived by:	Women	Men	Women	Men	Women	Men	Women	Men
'Womanly' Attributes								
Likely to get on if good looking	68	82	50	46	93	92	85	85
Like to be romantically involved	91	94	94	91	96	97	95	94
Want to settle and have a family	99	97	95	94	87	91	66	70
Need to be gentle and affectionate	89	93	74	69	84	87	56	52
Could not survive without the other sex	77	76	84	77	62	73	80	75
Averages:	84.8	88.4	79.6	75.4	84.4	88.0	76.4	75.2
'Manly' Attributes								
Get on well with own sex	85	79	96	95	59	64	86	87
Successfully hold own against own sex	76	80	91	90	85	84	91	91
Interested in politics	56	42	84	82	42	31	83	77
Need a good job to justify lives	38	34	85	85	57	49	91	91
Need to feel they dominate other sex	32	40	81	75	51	51	88	81
Averages:	57.4	55.0	87.4	85.4	58.8	55.8	87.8	85.4
Differences between upper and lower averages	27.4	33.4	−7.8	−10.0	25.6	32.2	−11.4	−10.2

Note: Survey conducted in Yorkshire ITV region.

Table 2. Percentages of female and male respondents who perceived each characteristic as true of women and men in real life and on TV.

Those evaluated: Perceived by:	REAL LIFE				TELEVISION			
	Women		Men		Women		Men	
	Women	Men	Women	Men	Women	Men	Women	Men
'Womanly' Attributes								
Likely to get on if good looking	67	79	44	56	97	94	90	85
Like to be romantically involved	93	88	92	90	96	88	94	93
Want to settle and have a family	100	97	93	85	86	85	66	66
Need to be gentle and affectionate	85	84	68	61	80	83	50	51
Could not survive without the other sex	52	77	82	80	64	71	82	77
Averages:	79.4	85.0	75.8	74.4	84.6	84.2	76.4	74.4
'Manly' Attributes								
Get on well with own sex	85	76	96	95	58	55	84	81
Successfully hold own against own sex	69	69	89	88	79	86	96	92
Interested in politics	50	45	87	80	45	34	81	78
Need a good job to justify lives	49	43	87	82	49	48	93	
Need to feel they dominate other sex	26	48	84	69	41	62	85	84
Averages:	55.8	56.2	88.6	82.8	54.4	57.0	87.8	84.7
Differences between upper and lower averages	23.6	28.8	-12.8	-8.4	30.2	27.2	-11.4	-10.3

Note: Survey conducted in the Central Scotland ITV region

thy differences. People thought women in particular, but also men, were shown as likely to get on well if they were good looking on television, much more often than they felt applied in real life. Women respondents were less likely to say that women in real life needed to be good-looking to get on, than were men. Both sexes thought television underplayed males' need to be gentle and affectionate compared with what they considered was true in real life.

With regard to more 'manly' attributes, the overall perceptions were that they applied more to men than to women, and to a similar extent both on television and in real life. Again though, there were particular item differences; women were more likely than men to notice that women in real life might be interested in politics, and this perceived difference applied as well with regard to their perceptions of the portrayal of women's interest in politics on television.

Overall, men respondents in both these British surveys showed a slightly greater polarisation in attributing characteristics to women, both on television and in real life, than did women respondents. While men again showed slightly more polarisation than women in linking more male and female characteristics to real life men, this did not occur in men's description of television portrayals of man. Many of the inter-respondent cross-contextual and sex-role related differences are significant and tests for these significance levels have been reported elsewhere (Gunter, 1984). The cross-contextual differences in particular raise an important question; for if perceivers can and do recognise that television portrayal differs from real life and people are in contact with the latter, there is no need for them to infer that television portrayal is an accurate picture of real life. In short, if people recognise television is different, this may insulate them from the 'short circuits' of perception that are implied in the 'cultivation effects' theory referred to earlier.

Summary

The description of sex-role portrayals on television as highly stereotyped is not consistently reinforced by the perceptions of viewers. Furthermore, the characteristics identified as typical of female or male portrayals on television by content analyses are

42

not necessarily ones which turn out to be the most salient to the audience.

Although audience perceptions of the sexes on television do not exhibit a consistent pattern throughout, one significant finding is that viewers do not seem passively to absorb everything they see on television. Perceptions of characters and behaviours appear to be mediated by pre-existing dispositions. Thus, boys often pay more attention to male characters than to female charaters, while girls pay relatively more attention to females than do boys, although they may still be attracted to some male characters more than they are to most female characters on the screen.

On the question of whether viewers perceive sex-role portrayals as sexist or not, as content analysis research has indicated they are, again the findings reveal a level of sophistication among members of the audience that is so often underestimated. On some attributes audience perceptions reinforce the content descriptions of the way women and men are shown, whilst on other attributes, the two kinds of judgement do not match. One thing that has emerged from recent audience research, however, is that even if television's sex-role portrayals are seen, on some dimensions, as stereotyped, beliefs about the sexes in real life may be quite different.

Chapter 4

Social effects of television and sex stereotyping

The evidence linking television sex stereotyping with public attitudes and behaviours derives from two research perspectives both of which are faced with problems of methodology and theoretical interpretation of data. Some of the evidence is correlational; such studies examine the relationship between the amount of time spent with television and the degree to which viewers hold certain sex-type attitudes or engage in sex-typed behaviours. While correlational data can offer useful indications of where relationships between variables may lie, they do not establish that one event causes another.

The second form of evidence derives from experimental studies conducted under laboratory conditions designed to facilitate the demonstration of cause-effect relationships. Under these conditions, researchers have greater control over the kinds of programmes and portrayals that are shown to and seen by groups of viewers. Problems occur, however, when attempting to generalise from television effects measured under these artificially contrived conditions of viewing to possible effects outside the laboratory under natural conditions of television exposure.

Research with adults

Gerbner and Signorielli (1979) examined patterns of television viewing among adults and correlated them with answers to a series of questions measuring sexist attitudes. They reported positive relationships between amount of viewing and beliefs that women should stay at home and that a woman should not work if her husband can support her.

These findings were explained in terms of television influence upon sex-role attitudes. This interpretation must be treated with caution however, since more than one explanation would be consistent with the data. Does television viewing cause sexist attitudes, or do these relationships indicate that people with sexist attitudes watch more television than less sexist people?

Volgy and Schwartz (1980) reported higher levels of sexism among adults heavily exposed to television entertainment programmes, although doubts have been cast on their results in view of the flimsy measures employed (see Hawkins and Pingree, 1982). Two years later, Rose, Anderson and Wisocki (1982) reported finding a significant relationship among college students between how they described themselves on an inventory designed to measure sex-typing and the amount of television they said they watched. The amount of sex-stereotyping in self-descriptions was positively correlated with amount of claimed viewing of programmes that had been previously rated by the researchers as strongly stereotyped in their portrayals of the sexes.

Other American researchers have suggested that the nature of television's influence on beliefs about women and men varies across different population subgroups. The relationship between television viewing and sex-stereotyping may not be a straightforward linear one in the same direction across all viewers, whereby sexism grows stronger with heavier viewing. Instead, there is evidence to suggest that television-sexism relationships work in opposite ways across different population subgroups. According to one line of argument, television cultivates a common level of sexist orientation, causing those who are less stereotyped or traditional in their beliefs about women's roles to become more so, and those who are strongly sexist in their beliefs to become less so (Gerbner and Signorielli, 1979).

British research has produced less conclusive evidence of systematic relationships between television viewing and beliefs about the sexes indicative of television cultivation effects among adults. IBA research by Gunter and Wober (1982) reported a study that was concerned not simply with relationships between total television viewing and beliefs about women and men, but also with the way these perceptions were associated with particular patterns of programme watching. Since different programmes portray women and men in different ways, do individuals who watch a great deal of one type of programme hold different beliefs about each sex than individuals who watch more of another type of programme? And if such patterns of relationships do exist between programme preferences and beliefs, are they to be interpreted as evidence of selective viewing or specific television influences? A further question investigated by this research related to the assumption by some writers that television cultivates sex-stereotyping as audiences assimilate traditionalist messages about the nature and roles of the sexes, conveyed explicitly or implicitly by programmes. Subjective perceptions of male and female television characters may often differ from the character profiles painted by objective content analysis. An important comparison, largely missed by most researchers, is whether viewers' perceptions of the sexes as seen on television are the same as their perceptions of the sexes in real life, and whether both sets of perceptions relate in similar ways to patterns and preferences of television viewing.

In the Gunter and Wober study, diary measures of television viewing were related to questionnaire responses concerning the way women were seen first on television and secondly in real life. The questionnaire was in three parts. In the first part, respondents were asked to say how true or untrue it was that women on television in daily life serials (e.g., soap operas), in situation comedies, or in advertisements are portrayed as 'not being interested in politics', 'wanting at some time to be mothers', 'quarrelsome with other women', 'very interested in jobs and careers', 'very keen on romantic affairs with men', 'depending on men to help them out of trouble', and 'more likely to get on if attractive'. In the second part, respondents were required to say how true or untrue each of these items was of women in real life; and in the final part, slightly re-worded versions of these items were presented concerning the way women *ought* to lead their lives. These items were chosen to reflect common characteristics or roles portrayed by women on television which had been previously identified by content analysis studies, and which supposedly functioned to cultivate sexist prototypes among viewers (see Lemon, 1978; Tuchman, 1978; Butler and Paisley, 1980).

From their completed viewing diaries, respondents were scored for the total number of programmes viewed during the survey week and for amount of viewing of several programme types: serious action-drama (consisting of crime-detective series and feature films), soap operas, comedy shows, and news and current affairs prorammes. Respondents were then divided into light, medium and heavy viewers of television in general and of each of these programme types.

Special statistical tests were computed to assess the strength of the relationships between television viewing patterns and beliefs about women, which controlled at the same time for any differences in viewing or in perceptions that might be due to the sex, age or class of respondents. These analyses revealed a number of significant relationships between television viewing and perceptions of women as seen on television and in real life, but only with respect to viewing of serious action-drama programming. There were no relationships between perceptions and total amount of television viewing.

Significant relationships emerged between amount of serious action-drama viewing and endorsements of how women are portrayed on television, how they appear in real life, and how they should be in real life on four attributes: 'women as interested in jobs and careers', 'women as keen on romantic affairs with men', 'women dependent on men to help them out of trouble' and 'women as getting on better if they are attractive'. Further significant relationships emerged between serious action-drama viewing and perceptions that 'women want to be mothers' in real life and that they 'should want to be mothers'. With respect to women as seen on television, viewing behaviour was related only to perceptions of female portrayals in daily life serials (i.e., serious dramas with a continuing story-line from one week to the next), and was unrelated to perceptions of women in situation comedies or advertisements on television.

The results showed that heavy viewers of serious action and drama programmes were significantly less likely than light viewers to perceive that women are portrayed in serious drama serials as interested in jobs and careers, keen on romantic affairs with men, dependent on men to help them out of trouble, and as getting on if they are attractive.

There were also five attributes of real life women on which perceptions were related to amount of serious action-drama viewing. Heavy viewers of this type of programming were less likely to say that women are keen on romantic affairs. Heavy action viewers also perceived women in everyday life as less career-orientated, and less often than did light action viewers as dependent on men when in trouble or as dependent on their own attractiveness in getting on.

Further analyses revealed that viewing behaviour was also significantly related to opinions on the same five attributes concerning perceptions of how women *should be ideally* in real life. These results indicated that heavy viewers of serious action-drama programmes were less likely to agree that women should want to become mothers or that they should be interested in sexual relations as much as men. Heavy action-drama viewers were also more likely than light viewers, however, to feel that women should be interested in jobs and careers, and that they should be self-reliant when faced with problems, rather than depending on men to help them out of trouble. Heavy action-drama viewers also were less likely than were light action viewers to feel that women should get on well with other women and that women should be judged on abilities rather than looks.

Content analysis studies have, over the years, identified a number of prominent images of women on television and inferred that, through regular viewing of these, stereotyped beliefs about women are cultivated amongst the general public. The results from the present study afforded the opportunity to examine actual public perceptions of female portrayals on television *and* to see whether or not these perceptions corres- ponded with the 'images' of women defined through content analysis.

In serious dramas, content studies have indicated that women are portrayed mainly in domestic, familial roles, and much less often in professional career-orientated roles. Women are often shown as preoccupied with romance and as dependent on men to help them whenever they get into trouble, especially outside the home (see Seggar and Wheeler, 1973; Lemon, 1978; Tuchman, 1978). Perceptions of women on television serials obtained from viewers, however, did not indicate strong tendencies for viewers to see women as wanting to be mothers, preoccupied by romance, or depending on men when in trouble. Viewers' subjective perceptions on these attributes did not coincide with the 'images' of television women which had been identified by objective content analysis. Agreement between viewers' perceptions and objectively coded qualities of women did occur on the item concerning women shown as interested in jobs and careers (Gunter and Wober, 1982).

There was no consistent evidence across attributes of relative differences in perceptions of women on television by light and heavy viewers of serious dramas that corresponded with inferences about the cultivation of stereotyped beliefs derived from content analysis. Heavy viewers of serious action-drama actually perceived women in television serials as more independent of men rather than as less independent as would be predicted by content analysis. There was no marked relationship between amount of action-drama viewing and perceptions of television women as wanting to be mothers and settled with a family, even though content analyses have often indicated that this is the way women are shown (Tedesco, 1974; Tuchman, 1978). Heavy viewers of serious action-drama were less likely than light viewers of these programmes to perceive women on television as career-orientated, and on this one item, audience perceptions actually corresponded with content analytic descriptions of the way women are portrayed (see Butler and Paisley, 1980).

Another important question is whether viewing behaviour relates to perceptions of women in real life, and also whether real-life perceptions are consistent with television perceptions of women. Gunter and Wober's study found that beliefs about women being interested in careers, being keen on romance, being dependent on men when in trouble and needing to be attractive to get on were each related to action-drama viewing for television and real-life perceptions. But how consistent in direction were these relationships?

Heavy action-drama viewers perceived women on television serials as not interested in jobs and careers more than did light-action viewers and also believed that this is the way women *are* and *should be* in real life. In addition, heavy action-drama viewers perceived women as less keen on romance on television and in reality, and believed that they should not be preoccupied by sexual relations with men in everyday life. There was an inverse relationship between amount of serious action-drama viewing and the belief that attractiveness was an essential feature for television women to get on and that women relied heavily on their attractiveness to make progress in life. Heavy action-drama viewers also tended to believe, more than did light viewers, that women should not be judged on looks alone. Finally, heavy action-drama viewers perceived women as dependent on men in television serials or in real life less than did light viewers, and believed more that women should be self-reliant. Clearly, there is consistency in the beliefs held about women as they are depicted on the television screen in certain programmes and as they appear in real life, although these beliefs do not always match the images of women on television identified by objective content analysis.

Research with children

Research has established that children know what sex they are by between a year-and-a-half and three years of age (Money and Ehrhardt, 1973), but do they also begin to limit their life options because of a mental association between role and sex? Content analyses have indicated that one of the most prevalent areas in which sex-role stereotyping occurs on television is with respect to employment (Butler and Paisley, 1980; Downing, 1974; Tedesco, 1974). To what extent does this content influence children's perceptions of the kind of job to which they will be most suited in later life?

Studies of television's influence on sex stereotyping among children have so far produced mixed results. In a small number of correlational analyses, some researchers have reported no significant relationships between personal or parental estimates of children's television viewing and their sex-role perceptions, whilst others have reported significant degrees of association which have been interpreted as evidence for a television influence.

In one study with 11–12 year-old children, both the children's and parents' sex-role perceptions were assessed along with the children's television viewing. (Perloff, 1977). No significant relationship emerged between the numbers of hours per week children watched television and the degree of stereotyping in their sex-role perceptions. However, parental sexism was marginally related to stereotyping among children. Children whose mothers went out to work, for example, were less stereotyped.

The above findings were reinforced in another survey (Meyer, 1980) among 15 girls aged 6–8 years and 10–12 years for whom, once again, amount of television viewing was related statistically to a range of attitudes and beliefs about the sexes. Neither personal nor parental estimates of television viewing were significantly related to children's attitudes. A more important influence than television upon children's sex-role attitudes were the attitudes of their mothers.

Finally, in a study done by Cheles-Miller (1975) the degree of acceptance among 9-10 year-old children of traditionally sex-stereotyped beliefs about marital roles for men and women as portrayed in television commercials was found to be greater among lighter viewers of television than among heavier viewers.

Some researchers have reported significant statistical relationships between television exposure and children's sex-role perceptions, without reference to viewing of specific types of content. Beuf (1974) conducted interviews with children of both sexes between the ages of three and six, asking them what they would like to be when they grew up. As well as specific questions about television viewing habits, each child was asked, 'What do you want to be when you grow up?' Then they were required to imagine what they would be if they were a member of the opposite sex. Thus, boys were asked, 'If you were a girl, what would you be when you grow up?' Finally, the children were engaged in a game called 'The OK Picture Game' in which they were shown several pictures, some of which were quite ordinary scenes of situations and others of which depicted something unusual or out of place, such as a five-legged cat. The interviewer explained to the children that the object of the game was to see whether a picture was 'OK' or not. Among several 'dummy' pictures were three scenes in which traditional sex roles had been reversed — a father feeding a baby, a man pouring coffee for a woman, and a female telephone-line repair person.

Results on career aspirations indicated a strong relationship between sex and envisaged future occupations for both own-sex and other-sex conditions. Boys tended to nominate traditionally 'masculine' professions such as policeman, sports star or cowboy; girls preferred quieter occupations such as nursing. While the actual jobs nominated by girls and boys were different, the tendency to stereotype career aspirations was virtually the same for both sexes. Over 70 percent of boys and 73 percent of the girls chose stereotypical careers for themselves. Even when asked what they would be if they were a member of the opposite sex, in nearly all cases, these youngsters selected what is normally regarded as appropriate for that sex.

Responses to pictures indicate that sex-typing increased as images moved from child-care to husband-wife roles to occupations. The children's beliefs reflected the increasing post-war trends of husbands helping around the house. However, regardless of the growing women's liberation movement, children still showed strong sex-typing with respect to occupational roles; whilst young children's sex-role perceptions measured here indicated strong stereotyping of ideas about the sexes, to what extent are they affected by television portrayals?

Beuf claims that sex stereotyping of career aspirations was more likely to occur among heavier viewers of television, but she presents no data to back up this assertion. Furthermore, Beuf's sample was small and unrepresentative of this age-band and her findings need to be replicated with other groups of children before they can be confidently accepted.

In a subsequent study, Frueh and McGhee (1975) obtained personal and parental estimates of television viewing for kindergarten, second, fourth and sixth grade children, and then presented them with a projective measure of sex-role stereotyping. The latter was a paper and pencil test which examined children's choice of sex-typed toys. Strength of traditional sex-role beliefs showed a clear, positive association with amount of television viewing. Frueh and McGhee also found that boys and older children made the greatest number of traditionally sex-typed choices on the test. The conclusion of the study is that children learn about traditional sex roles from television. A number of critical questions remain unanswered however. Why were boys and older children more traditional in their attitudes? Was it their traditional attitudes that made some children heavier television viewers in the first place? What role did parents play, not only in teaching children about sex roles, but also in helping them to interpret what was seen on television? How accurate was parental monitoring of actual viewing among the youngest children? Was the sample of forty girls and forty boys representative of their age groups? Was the projective test a valid measure of children's sex role development?

In a follow up study, McGhee (1975) and McGhee and Frueh (1980) reported further research they had conducted with the same children 15 months after their initial contact with them. On this occasion the researchers were interested to find out whether heavy television watchers (those watching 25 hours or more per week) differed from light television watchers (those watching 10 hours or less per week) among different age-groups in their adoption over time of sex-stereotyped beliefs.

McGhee (1975) reported results from two different measures of sex-role stereotyping which were related in opposite directions to the amount of television viewing claimed for children. On the basis of measures obtained from the scale used in the Frueh and McGhee study, McGhee found that lighter television viewers only had become more stereotyped in their sex-role perspectives. Elsewhere, however, the validity of this scale as a measure of sex-stereotyping has been called into question and it has been claimed that it may be inadequate as such a measure with children over the age of seven years (Durkin, 1985).

With the second scale, however, sex-role stereotyping was found to be stronger among heavier television viewers. It is difficult to disentangle these findings and to know which ones are more accurate. Consistent with earlier findings, McGhee and Frueh, in a further paper, reported that heavy viewers held more stereotyped perceptions than did light viewers. It also emerged, however, that the perception of male stereotypes steadily declined with increasing age among light viewers, while among heavy viewers these stereotypes were maintained with increasing age. No comparable results were obtained for stereotyped perceptions of females. The authors hypothesised that television may reinforce and maintain sex-stereotyped perceptions among heavy viewers, while light viewers, who presumably spend more time gaining experience about people other than through television, do not exhibit such strong stereotypes.

This interpretation of their results by McGhee and Frueh conveniently overlooks a serious internal problem with their study. The scale on which sex-role stereotyping was measured consisted of two sub-scales — one contained items referring to perceptions of male attributes and the other of female attributes. In fact only responses to the male items were reported, which according to one other writer suggests that it was perhaps only on these items that sex–role perceptions were related to television viewing (Durkin, 1985b).

Further evidence has emerged of positive relationships between increased viewing of television and more stereotyped beliefs about the sexes. Zuckerman, Singer and Singer (1980) examined variations in sex-role prejudice as a function of television viewing, demographic characteristics and family background of children. They studied 155 North American children of average age nine and a half years. In general it was found that these children were not strongly stereotyped in their sex-role perceptions, but that where stereotyping did occur it was most evident among girls with lower IQs, who had mothers with higher educational attainment and who watched great amounts of television. The same results did not emerge among boys.

Perhaps the strongest correlational evidence that television viewing influences children's sex role attitudes so far comes from a longitudinal study of American adolescents (Morgan, 1980). Measures of television exposure (hours viewed in the 'average day'), acceptance of sex-role stereotypes and educational or occupational aspirations, were taken over the course of two years, and the method of cross-logged panel correlations was applied to the data. The results support the view that television inculcates certain sex-role views, although the effects are limited to girls. Television viewing in the first year of the

55

study significantly mediated girls' third-year attitudes; heavy viewers were more likely than light viewers to agree that men have more ambition than women, that women are happiest raising children, and so on. There was no evidence that early degree of sex-stereotyping among girls mediated subsequent television viewing patterns. Among boys, on the other hand, television appeared to have no manifest longitudinal impact on sex-role attitudes, but existing sexism foreshadowed greater viewing at a later date. Among girls also the effects of television were greater among the middle-classes. Both lower-class females and males generally were more sexist regardless of viewing levels. These findings suggested that television viewing is most likely to have an influence among those individuals who are least stereotyped in their views.

Morgan also reported, again for girls only, a relationship between amount of television viewing in the first year of measurement and subsequent educational and occupational aspirations. Interestingly, however, the heavier viewers were the ones who two years later set their sights *higher*. This result, although predicted by Morgan on the basis of television's over-representation of professional women, runs contrary to the traditional influences reported by most other studies.

Although on balance the tone of Morgan's interpretation of his findings points to a sex-role stereotyping effect of regular television watching, in fact careful observation of the details of Morgan's study reveals that his findings are complex and difficult to explain.

Correlations between television viewing and sex-role percep-tions were made at and across two points in time and were compared not only between boys and girls but also between three (high, medium and low) IQ groups. Television viewing was significantly related to sexism only among medium IQ boys and high IQ girls. No explanation is provided for the result among the boys, whilst the correlations among the girls were interpreted as evidence for television's influence, on the assumption that girls with high IQs are less likely to be sexist in the first place. Unfortunately, the small magnitude of his correlations does not provide strong evidence on which confidently to assume an effect of television (Durkin, 1985b).

Mention should be made at this point of a recently published study from Canada which took advantage of a naturally occurring situation in a community which at the outset consisted of an essentially television-naive population (Kimball, 1986; Williams, 1986).

Surveys were carried out in three communities both before and two years after television reception was introduced for the first time to one of the towns. The other two towns were able to receive one and four television channels respectively.

Children in all three communities were administered scales to measure their sex-role attitudes at both points in time. A set of Peer Scales asked children to rate how appropriate or frequent certain behaviours are for boys and girls their own age, and a set of Parent Scales asked children to rate how frequently their own mother and father perform certain tasks.

At the outset, children in the television-receiving towns were found to be much more stereotyped on peer ratings than were those children from the town with no television reception. Two years later, following the introduction of television to the latter community, children living there were found to have become significantly more stereotyped in their attitudes towards the sexes. This change was restricted to perceptions of peers, however; no similar impact was observed on ratings of parents.

Kimball concluded that in the longer term television has the potential to shape children's sex-role attitudes and recommended that more women should be presented on television. Special attention should be given to the way women are depicted.

A major problem with the above studies is that exposure to sex-stereotyping on television is measured purely in terms of gross viewing behaviour. It is assumed that a certain level of viewing *per se* will result in exposure to a great deal of the sex stereotyping, which content analysis studies have indicated is contained by television programmes. As we saw earlier, however, subjectively, viewers may not perceive portrayals and events in programmes as having the same characteristics as those described by objective coding analyses of television content. Furthermore, gross estimates of television viewing do not tell us whether viewers have actually seen programmes in which sex-role stereotyping is supposedly most commonplace. If overall television viewing does not relate to sex-role attitudes, is it because television has no effect or is it because it has more than one kind of effect, with one effect counterbalancing the other? In other words, if programmes contain stereotypical and counter-stereotypical portrayals of the sexes, are viewers' attitudes influenced by both types of portrayal in a complementary fashion? There is correlational evidence, and as we shall see in the next section experimental evidence, that the precise influence of television on sex-role attitudes may depend on the particular kinds of portrayals viewed.

An experimental study by Tan (1979) reinforced the correlational evidence for sex-stereotyping effects of watching sex-stereotyped television portrayals under more controlled conditions of television watching. Tan found that adolescent girls, fed a heavy dose of beauty advertisements were more likely than a control group of girls who did not see these advertisements to believe that being beautiful is an important female characteristic and is necessary to attract men. Twenty-three high-school girls, aged sixteen to eighteen years, viewed fifteen commercials which emphasised the desirability of sex appeal, beauty or youth (e.g., advertisements for soap, toothpaste, beauty products, etc) and thirty-three girls viewed commercials which contained no beauty messages (e.g., advertisements for dog food, soya sauce and diapers). Each girl was then asked to rank order the relative importance of ten attributes (e.g., pretty face, intelligence, sex appeal, hard-working, competence, etc) in each of four areas (career/job, wife, to be liked by men, and desirable personal attribute). The girls who saw the beauty advertisements ranked the importance of the beauty and sex-appeal qualities significantly higher than did the non-beauty advertisement group for the item 'to be liked by men' and with marginal significance in the same direction also for the item 'personally desirable'.

One recent British study by Gallagher (1983) describes a questionnaire survey carried out amongst a small sample of second- and third-year children at a single secondary school in Northampton, and with a smaller sample of parents of some of these children. In all, the findings derive from 235 usable questionnaires from the children and 92 filled out by parents. The sample was non-representative and most families were middle class. In most instances, fathers had professional managerial or skilled occupations and many of the mothers also went out to work.

Parents were questioned on their attitudes to men and women at work, and in the family, and about their aspirations for their children. Children were given a list of fifteen concepts including such items as Men, Women, Marriage, Having an Education, Intelligence, Me, Taking Care of Children, Housework, Having a Job, Being Responsible, etc. These were presented in pairs to the children who were required to say how much two items belonged together. This instrument was designed to measure children's sex-role stereotyping.

Among parents, results indicated that women and men in the sample held similar attitudes towards men and women at work or in the family context in some respects, and differed in levels of agreement on other attitudes. For example, both male and female respondents tended to agree that a married woman's most important task in life should be taking care of her husband and children. Both tended to disagree that if a husband and wife disagree about something, the husband should make the final decision. However, men were three times as likely as women to say that a woman, unlike a man, does not need to make a long-term career plan for her future.

All parents had high educational and career aspirations for their children although occupational aspirations tended to be stronger for sons than for daughters.

From their judgements about men and women using the fifteen sex-role concepts, children showed that they perceived Close Relationships between Women, Taking Care of Children and Housework, and between Having an Education, Intelligence, and the self-concept Me. Boys tended to perceive much more distance than did girls between the self-concept Me and concepts such as Housework, Taking Care of Children, Marriage, Showing Emotion and Being Obedient. Thus, many of the boys' and girls' perceptions indicated traditional stereotyping of sex-role beliefs.

On the relationship between television viewing and sex-role attitudes and perceptions, Gallagher correlated respondents' own estimates of amount of time spent viewing each week with questionnaire responses. She found that men and women who held more 'traditional' sex-role attitudes tended to watch more television than those who held more 'egalitarian' attitudes. However, traditional attitudes and heavier viewing were both also associated with level of education and self-perceived intelligence. Unfortunately no appropriate statistical controls were employed for these additional variables in the presence of which the relationship between attitudes and viewing might have been weakened or reduced to non-significance.

Gallagher also reported positive relationships between 'traditional' sex-role perceptions among girls and boys and the amount of television they claimed to watch. But once again she failed to allow for other important factors such as parental attitudes which might have been explicitly or implicitly passed on to their children, or the extent to which parents shared household chores (which related independently to egalitarian perceptions amongst children).

Summary

Early research on the effects of sex-role portrayals on television on the audience's beliefs about women and men suggested a link between the two. Among children, for instance, those youngsters who were categorised as heavy viewers were found to hold stronger beliefs than did lighter viewers in what research defined as a stereotyped direction. Much of this work, however, failed to provide precise measures of what young viewers had actually watched. Further, these studies did not consider what kind of sense viewers made of the things they saw on the screen, when we know from research evidence elsewhere that viewers' perceptions of the sexes on television are quite complex.

The model adopted by effects researchers has usually been one in which television is assumed to act upon a passively receptive audience. This model we now know to be oversimplistic. Viewers exhibit a degree of activity in selecting what to watch on television, what to pay attention to, and what to remember of the things which pass before their eyes on the small screen. Even children respond in a selective fashion to particular characters and events on television, and their perceptions, memories and understanding of what they have seen may often be mediated by dispositions they bring with them to the viewing situation.

Until individual differences in the psychological make-up of viewers (young and old), in their choices of what to watch, and their perception and comprehension of what they have seen on television are included in research concerned with television's effects in this context, we can not hope fully to understand the extent and nature of television's impact on beliefs about the sexes.

Chapter 5

Counter-stereotyping
through television

There is a tendency among mass communications researchers, which has become almost a tradition, to look only or at least primarily for the negative effects of television. This can be seen quite clearly from the vast funds and resources that have been invested in research on the impact of televised violence. And it is illustrated further in the sex-role development literature by the emphasis that is placed on television's cultivation of stereotyped beliefs about the sexes which tend to be more favourable for men than for women.

Considerably less attention and investment of research resources have been directed at exploring and developing the potential of television to contribute instrumentally and positively towards a broadening of social attitudes about the sexes. Recently, however, in a movement away from this negative tradition, several studies have emerged which have begun to explore the efficacy of television as an instrument for opening up attitudes and perceptions concerning the roles of women and men in society. There are indications from early studies that televised examples of counter-stereotyped portrayal which break away from the traditional portrayals of women and men may produce positive changes in the variety of expectations young viewers come to hold for their own and the opposite sex.

Much of the content analytic literature reviewed earlier in this monograph pointed to pronounced stereotyping in the way women and men were portrayed on television. Typically, men get to play a greater variety of more interesting and more powerful roles than women. In recent years however, this pattern has begun to change. A new kind of leading female figure has begun to emerge who is independent, competent, and career-minded and is every bit equal, if not superior, to the men around her (e.g., Jamie Summers in the *Bionic Woman*, Chris Cagney in *Cagney and Lacey*, Maggie Forbes in *C.A.T.s Eyes*, Dee Dee McCall in *Hunter*, Diana Prince in *Wonder Woman*).

American evidence has indicated that preschool girls seem to identify with this new breed of heroine. At the same time, it has been observed that girls of this age seem to be more assertive and aggressive than those in earlier studies conducted before such characters appeared on peak-time television (Singer and Singer, 1981). Of course, to lay responsibility for these apparent behavioural changes at the door of television is probably overshooting the mark. Broader changes in public attitudes concerning female roles in modern society, perhaps passed on to the child by his/her parents, undoubtedly play a major part in the sex-role attitudes and behaviour of young children (see Cheles-Miller, 1975; Perloff, 1977). But the role of television in influencing attitude changes which go against the traditional 'grain' ought not to be ignored.

In this section, we turn our attention to research concerned with the countering of traditional sex stereotypes through televised examples of alternative social roles for men and women. Although we are still concerned in a general sense with the effects of television on sex-role perceptions, the separation of research on *counter*-stereotyping effects from research on stereotyping effects is an important theoretical distinction. These two kinds of effects cannot be assumed to be of the same kind. The influence of television on what are termed 'traditional' perceptions of the sexes cannot easily be differentiated from the influences of other sources of information about men and women which also typically carry traditionalist messages. Furthermore, there is every likelihood that portrayals which run counter to traditional stereotypes may not be reacted to in the same way as traditional portrayals by viewers. Their novel and unusual character may make counter-stereotyped portrayals particularly salient. On the other hand, their relative rarity may mean that the influence of counter-stereotypes and even the ability of viewers to retain them in memory, may be swamped by the overwhelming tide of traditionalism which supposedly characterises sex-role portrayals on television (see Durkin, 1985c). Let us now turn to the evidence for the counter-stereotyping effects of television on sex-role portrayals.

Miller and Reeves (1976) conducted a survey of adolescent school children to assess the differential impact on ex-role beliefs of viewing programmes classified as stereotyped or non-stereotyped in the way they portrayed the sexes. The researchers began with the fact that objective content analyses of US television programmes had indicated that men and women are depicted differently on a number of social dimensions. For example, women are less likely than men to be employed, more likely to be married, more likely to hold jobs which are less varied and have lower status, and so on. They then located five programmes which countered this social profile, showing women in traditionally male occupations and other social roles, and measured the extent of viewing these shows. Their results revealed a strong positive association between frequency of viewing counter-stereotypical programmes and young viewers' sense that it was 'OK' for girls to aspire to the kinds of non-typical roles portrayed in these shows — school principal, police officer, park ranger and TV producer. Boys and girls were equally accepting of non-traditional aspirations as a consequence.

Experimentalists have been concerned not only with the effects of viewing certain kinds of television on sex-stereotyping but have also examined the potential of television, through the portrayal of the sexes in non-traditional roles, to cultivate counter-stereotypic beliefs about men and women. It is only under the degrees of viewing control provided by experiments that the specific effects of viewing these different types of sex-role portrayal can be effectively measured. Experimental research among adult and child viewers has indicated not only that sex stereotyping on television can promote or reinforce such stereotypes, but also that counter-stereotyped portrayals can have the reverse effect.

Research with adults

One difficulty in testing the effects of media sex-role stereotyping on sex-role learning and sex-role behaviour is that of locating a control which has never been exposed to stereotyped media portrayals. Jennings, Geis and Brown (1980) sought to overcome this problem by testing a contrast hypothesis. Rather than testing the hypothesis that stereotyped commercials depress women's self-confidence and independence of judgement, they tested the opposite of this, that commercials which *break* sex-role stereotyping raise women's self-confidence and independence of judgement. Jennings et al showed female college students traditional and non-traditional television commercials and found that those who saw non-traditional depictions of women subsequently expressed more career aspirations than those who saw traditional sex-stereotyped commercials. Building on these findings, the researchers investigated whether commercials could have effects, not only on the attitudes of female college students, but also on their behaviour.

Eight television commercials were devised; four showed women in traditional, dependent and subservient roles vis-à-vis men; the other four exactly reversed the roles within the same scenarios and showed women as dominant and men as subservient. After viewing one or the other set, viewers were questioned about the female and male roles shown. Then, half were given an Asch type conformity test. In this, they were asked to rate cartoons and were shown a set of falsified ratings supposedly supplied previously by other people. The degree to which their own opinions differed from the falsified ratings was interpreted as a measure of independence of judgement. Other participants in the experiment were asked to give a short, impromptu speech, and their degree of confidence in so doing was rated.

Those women who had seen the role-reversed commercials were more independent in their ratings of cartoons and more self-confident in giving a speech than were those who had seen the stereotyped versions. Given the absence of any similarity between the nature of the commercials and of the subsequent situations in which they were to perform, it is unlikely that the observed behavioural effects arose from the explicit content of the advertisements. Indeed the women were, it seems, unaware of the influence exercised by the commercials. Moreover, when the women were asked if they identified with the people in the commercials, all reported a low level of identification regardless of the version seen. Nevertheless, there was an apparent behavioural effect which led the authors to point to an implicit message power in the commercials, assimilated by viewers unwittingly.

Geis, Brown, Jennings (Walstedt), and Porter (1984) asserted that sex stereotypes implicitly enacted, but not explicitly articulated, in television advertisements may inhibit women's achievement aspirations. To test for this effect, groups of men and women were shown either four television advertisements in which sex-stereotyping occurred, or four advertisements that were exactly the same except that the sex roles in them were reversed, or no advertisements at all. Afterwards, all who took part wrote an essay imagining their lives '10 years from now'. The essays were coded for achievement and home-making themes and comparisons were made across experimental groups. The results showed that women who had viewed the traditional sex-stereotyped advertisements de-emphasised achievement in favour of homemaking, compared to men generally, and compared to women who had seen the reversed role advertisements. The reversed role ads apparently had eliminated the sex difference in net achievement focus of the essays. Those individuals who did not see any advertisements at all were indistinguishable in the essay themes they emphasised from their same sex counterparts who saw the traditional sex-role advertisements.

Research with children

Experimental research on the influence of non-traditional sex-role portrayals has provided some indication of a reduction in stereotyping among young viewers who have seen them. Atkin and Miller (1975), for example, showed 400 children, aged between six and ten years, a fifteen-minute videotape of children's programmes consisting of a news show, a cartoon, and several commercials. One of the commercials was for eye glasses and featured a woman modelling glasses, who, in versions shown to three different groups of children, was portrayed either as a judge, a computer programmer, or a television technician. A fourth group of children saw no commercials at all. After the television presentation, the children were given a list of jobs and asked to indicate which ones they thought would be suitable employment for women. Seeing the woman in the commercial as a computer programmer or television technician did not affect judgements of the suitability of either of these jobs for women relative to not seeing the commercial, but seeing a female judge made children more likely to endorse this as an appropriate occupation for women (51 percent versus 31 percent for those who did not see this version). Girls and older children were most strongly influenced in this respect. There was also evidence of a generalisation of non-traditional beliefs to other occupations. Children who saw the female judge were also more likely to think that women could be doctors. Flerx, Fidler and Rogers (1976) found that five-year-olds who saw a film depicting men and women in non-traditional roles produced significant changes in beliefs about 'working mothers', 'nurturing fathers', and the kinds of games and activities appropriate for girls and boys.

McArthur and Eisen (1976) carried out a content analysis of male and female characters in children's Saturday morning television programmes and subsequently conducted an experiment to examine the effects on children's behaviour of watching stereotyped and non-stereotyped sex-role portrayals. The content analyses revealed that males and females were portrayed in different roles on children's television, they manifested different behaviours, and their behaviours were followed by different consequences. Male characters appeared on screen more often and were more active than females.

In the experiment which followed, pre-school children were shown short videotaped vignettes which depicted an adult male and female model engaging in a number of activities. Under one condition the models behaved in ways normally associated with their sex, while in a second version they reversed their activities to perform non-sex-typical behaviours. It was found that children tended to recall and reproduce more of the behaviours of a same-sex than of an opposite-sex television mode. This occurred even when the same-sex model displayed behaviours normally not thought of as associated with his or her own sex. Thus, boys were more likely to remember and imitate nurturant, domestic and artistic behaviours than leadership, bravery and problem-solving activities of a television model when the former behaviours were performed by a male and the latter by a female. On the other hand, when the sex of the models performing each set of activities fits current sex-role stereotypes, so did the boys' behaviour. Similar results were obtained for girls, although their tendency to show more imitations of a same-sex model was weaker than for boys.

Davidson, Yasina and Towers (1979) showed a group of five-year-old girls one of three cartoon shows. One cartoon showed a girl in a counter-stereotyped way, successfully behaving in various traditionally male pursuits including sports and building a clubhouse. Another cartoon showed a girl in a stereotyped fashion, and the third paid no particular attention to sex roles. The reverse-stereotyped version produced significantly less sex-stereotyping of personality characteristics than the other two programmes, although as the authors admit, it is impossible to know for sure which of many differences, both related and unrelated to sex-role perceptions, among the programmes, were responsible for producing the effects.

In another study, television commercial portrayals were used to influence children's sex-role attitudes. Pingree (1978) presented seven to nine-year-olds with television commercials showing either traditional or non-traditional female characterisations. In addition, children's perceptions of the reality of the commercials were manipulated, too, with instructions either that the characters were all real people or that they were all acting, or that the commercials were just like the ones seen at home (neutral). Children's perceptions of reality were successfully manipulated; children in the reality-set condition believed the commercial portrayals to be more realistic than did those in the acting-set condition, with children not given specific indications about the reality of the portrayals falling in between the latter two groups.

The overall effects of traditional and non-traditional presentations of women on attitudes were contradictory. Children who saw the commercials did not differ significantly in their attitudes towards women from a control group who saw no commercials.

However, for children who received instructions about the reality of the commercials, attitudes towards women were less traditional after viewing non-traditional commercials. Non-traditional portrayals had no effect on children's attitudes towards women when no specific instructional set was provided. It seems likely that the duration of this sequence of commercials (five minutes) was too brief to effect attitude change unless something else was done to heighten their impact — such as saying that they depicted real people.

The most elaborate and extensive study of the influence of television in sex-role stereotyping and counter-stereotyping is one reported by Johnston and Ettema (1982) concerning the 13-part television series *Freestyle*. This series was aimed at children in the nine to twelve year age range and attempted to convey a variety of counter-stereotyped lessons to young viewers. A total of 7000 children took part in the project across the United States. All children were pre and post tested with regard to their sex-role beliefs, attitudes and interests. Three areas of behaviour were focused on for change: children's pre-occupational activities (i.e., their interest and active involvement in activities of a mechanical or scientific nature that often lead on to specific careers later), behavioural skills (i.e., skills that children of this age begin to develop that are useful later on to the careers they decide to pursue), and adult work and family roles (including frequently stereotyped adult domestic and occupational roles). Viewing of the series took place under three different conditions. Some children viewed the programmes at school as a formal part of their curriculum and viewing was followed up by further discussion of the programmes, some children viewed in school but without further discussions, and other children were encouraged to watch the programme at home.

The results showed that viewing in school with discussion was the most successful condition for producing changes in beliefs and intended behaviours in a counter-stereotyped direction. Viewing in school without discussion produced certain changes in the same direction as the above but these were very much weaker. The viewing-at-home condition was the least effective.

The major changes included greater acceptance of girls who engage in athletics and mechanical activities, and who assume positions of leadership and display independence; greater acceptance of boys who engage in nurturing activities; and greater acceptance of men and women who choose non-traditional careers. Some children were tested after a delay of nine months following the end of the series. Many of the changes observed in the short term with the school viewing plus discussion condition, though somewhat weaker, nevertheless persisted and remained significantly different from pre-test measures.

Attempts to study the impact of televised examples of counter-stereotyping on children in Britain have been limited. Durkin (1983) reported two experimental studies, one with primary school children and the other with secondary school children. Both attempted to facilitate changes in the sex-role beliefs of young viewers using a single programme in which examples of non-stereotypic behaviour were depicted.

The first experiment with 52 primary school children used an edition of a programme called *Rainbow*. This programme had an introductory story and subsequent sketches, cartoons and song and dance sequences amplifying the theme. The story was about a conventional family consisting of the father, mother, son and daughter, which suffers an unfortunate event when the father is made redundant. The mother goes out to work instead and the father is left to take responsibility for household chores and looking after the children.

The children were randomly split up into three groups. One group saw *Rainbow*, one saw a programme about the weather, and a third group saw no programme at all. The youngsters' sex-role beliefs were measured both before and after viewing the programme by 16 questions concerning stereotypically male occupational roles (e.g., bus driver, doctor, farm worker), stereotypically female occupational roles (e.g., shop assistant, secretary, nurse), stereotypically male domestic roles (e.g., putting up shelves, cleaning the car), and stereotypically female domestic roles (e.g., cooking, ironing, shopping). The children were asked to indicate whether a man, a woman, or both could perform these roles. The test was administered for the first time about one week before the programme was viewed, and a second time within a day of viewing.

Both boys and girls in the *Rainbow* group changed their views

71

substantially. The *Rainbow* programme produced a short-term shift of opinion away from stereotyping. The programme seemed particularly effective in modifying children's beliefs about domestic roles. Durkin suggests that this may be because it may to some extent have alerted them to actual as opposed to stereotypical behaviour. Perhaps, many of these children already had fathers who helped with the dishes and shopping. After viewing, the children who watched *Rainbow* may have recalled these things more readily. The programme produced less change in beliefs about occupational roles however. And this may have been because for these children, such roles were still too far distant from their own experience and concerns for already well-established stereotyping to be changed by just one television programme.

In his second experiment, Durkin attempted to modify adolescents' career beliefs with specially prepared educational films. A total of 99 children aged 12 and 13 years participated in this exercise. They were divided into four groups. One group saw a film introducing traditional career opportunities; a second group saw a non-traditional opportunities film without any explicit attention being given in it to alternative careers for each sex (implicit counter-stereotype); a third group was shown a non-traditional opportunities film in which men and women discussed their occupations more openly (explicit counter-stereotype); and a fourth group saw no film.

The traditional film showed a male doctor, a female nurse, a male plumber and female secretary. The counter-stereotype films showed the same four occupations, but the actors were interviewed in pairs, one male and one female for each occupation. The difference between the implicit and explicit films was that in the latter more emphasis was placed on the reasons why particular actors had chosen a job not normally pursued by their sex.

Children in each group were given a list of 12 occupations consisting of four stereotypically male jobs, four stereotypically female jobs, and four 'neutral' jobs. They were asked to indicate in each case whether an occupation was 'just men's work', 'just women's work', or somewhere in between. The general finding was that children tended to rate male jobs as male, female jobs as female, and neutral jobs as neutral. There were very few differences between groups and therefore very little effect of experimental treatment. Even though the films were designed to offer career guidance, they seemed to have very little impact on children's existing stereotyped beliefs about occupations.

Chapter 6

Final remarks

Defining and measuring the effects of television on the public's images of women and men is a complex problem that can only be properly tackled through a multi-faceted research perspective which includes careful study of programmes, audiences, viewing behaviour, and viewers' perceptions of the things they see on television. The limitations of much of the research done so far are really to be found in the methods used. Most studies have been uni-dimensional, approaching the subject from one angle, employing one kind of measure and drawing conclusions which their measures do not entitle them to make. Many studies of television influence have used measures which lack any validity outside the research context or worse still are questionable even within that context. What then can be concluded from the research about the influence of television on sex-role stereotyping?

We began with a review of studies which looked at the way the sexes are depicted on the small screen. This research indicated that most television seems to be characterised by pronounced patterns of sex-stereotyping. This is manifested in a number of subtle ways. First of all, women are often numerically grossly outnumbered by men in many categories of programmes. Secondly, even in programmes where the numerical balance is restored, women appear to enjoy a much narrower range of roles than do men. Thirdly, certain personality characteristics tend to be overemphasised for women, and others for men, with the latter judged by researchers usually to possess the more favourable psychological profile. From these stereotyped patterns of male and female portrayals on television, many researchers have been tempted to infer certain effects of this content on viewers, assuming that such portrayals convey certain 'messages' to the audience about the sexes.

Whilst descriptive analyses of programmes may provide interesting catalogues of sex-role portrayals on television, problems arise when statements about the effects of these portrayals are derived from them in the absence of any supporting audience research. It is one thing to classify and describe the content of television programmes, but it is quite a different matter to establish that certain 'messages' or 'meanings' supposedly conveyed by television portrayals are being apprehended by viewers and absorbed into their existing belief systems. It is essential first of all to establish that viewers are taking certain meanings from the programmes they watch and secondly, to find out if their perceptions of programmes lead them to absorb the same 'messages' as those identified by the descriptive coding schemes of some researchers. In the absence of any empirical tests of audience perceptions and comprehension of programmes, such assumptions are pure conjecture.

Turning now to a model of how television's influence might operate on viewers' beliefs about the sexes in which an audience research component is included, we find that some writers have envisaged a process of influence whereby greater exposure *per se* to television's 'messages' produces greater television biased responding on items of belief about the way things are in the real world (e.g., Clark, 1972; Gerbner and Gross, 1976; Gerbner et al 1977).

The evidence offered to back up this hypothesis comes from correlational surveys in which measures of how much television people say they watch are correlated with their answers to certain attitudinal statements about men and women. Heavy viewers are assumed to be more heavily exposed to stereotyped portrayals of women and men on television than are light viewers, and therefore also to hold more stereotyped beliefs about women than the latter. Significant correlations between self-reported amounts of viewing and what are designated by the researchers as sex-stereotyped answers to questions about women and men, are taken as evidence for a television influence on sex-stereotyping (e.g., Beuf, 1974; Frueh and McGhee, 1975; McGhee and Frueh, 1980). But how much faith should we have in this evidence?

The safest answer probably is that such findings must be treated with caution. First of all, reliance on self-reports of fairly generalised estimates of television viewing of the sort which characterizes correlational studies may not actually be sufficient to provide accurate measures of exposure of viewers to stereotyped portrayals. The researchers who use these measures typically assume that heavy viewing of television means heavy exposure to such content, but this does not necessarily follow. Furthermore, the descriptive evidence indicates that sex-stereotyping, though consistently present, is not always consistent in style across different types of programmes. It could be therefore that heavy viewing of certain types of television results in heavy exposure to particular kinds of stereotyping and not others. Since not all heavy viewers will watch the same programmes, it may be important to know more about what they do watch before their endorsement of particular sex-role beliefs can be meaningfully linked to what they have seen on television.

A second problem is that of defining a sex-stereotyped belief. Researchers classify their respondents as 'sexist' on the basis of their answers to items of belief or opinion for which certain response options are pre-classified as stereotyped or non-stereotyped. But roles or characteristics deemed as most appropriate for men and women are defined by existing social norms. These norms do not remain constant, however, but change over time, so that what is regarded as acceptable behaviour for women today is not always the same as twenty years ago. Yet researchers seldom, if ever, base their definition of sex-stereotyping on surveys of normative social attitudes. With questions dealing with roles such as the kinds of occupations that women are best suited to, it may be relatively straightforward to distinguish between an open-minded (non-stereotypic) reply and a narrow-minded (stereotypic) one. But on questions of personality and character, it may be more problematic to make such a distinction. A descriptive study of television sex-role portrayals may conclude that women are typically shown as emotional creatures, but is this at odds with the way women are in real life? It may be shown that many women are pre-occupied by romantic relationships, or that their lives centre on their marriages and families, but is this not true of women (and men) in reality? Does television, across various categories of programming, play on these issues more or less than they actually occupy the attention of women and men in real life? And even if it does, we are left with the quite separate empirical question of the extent to which viewers accept or discuss television's scenarios and characterizations as conveyors of valuable lessons relevant to their own lives.

In addition to these problems, the interpretation of correlational relationships is always problematic anyway, and inferences of causal relations between sets of variables that are significantly correlated are usually fraught with ambiguity which is often extremely difficult to disentangle.

The problem of causality can be tackled more effectively via experimental designs. Experiments afford the advantage of greater control over the form and content of television stimulus materials and over the level of exposure to critical portrayals among different comparison groups of viewers. These studies suffer from typically small and non-representative samples, artificial conditions of viewing, and sometimes from measures of attitudinal and behavioural change which provide only poor indicators of television's capacity to produce psychological change in real life.

Furthermore, experimental studies on sex-role stereotyping or counter-stereotyping have so far demonstrated only short-term, simplistic changes in attitudes and beliefs concerning appropriate roles for each sex. They provide no conclusive proof that such effects occur in natural, everyday viewing environments and that such learning produces long-term change in the beliefs of individuals. What little experimental evidence there is of a possible long-term influence of television sex-role portrayals on viewers, sex-role beliefs in the realm of counter-stereotyping has indicated that televised examples alone may not be sufficient to influence viewers' perceptions.

In attempting to fashion changes in children's sex-role beliefs through a specially produced television series, Johnson and Ettema (1982) reported that such change depended crucially upon further, external reinforcement of the programmes' lessons about potential non-traditional roles for girls in the form of classroom discussions and written assignments about the programmes. Of course this study was attempting to produce shifts in beliefs in a counter-stereotypic direction. It could be reasoned that attempts to stem the tide of sex-stereotyping which pervades not only television but society in general, would require a concentrated, multi-channel approach. Where television sex-role portrayals are stereotyped, however, even single exposures whose individual effects are only short lasting, may, when repeated, add to the sex-stereotyped social conditioning process that touches practically everyone in society. Perhaps the crucial question at this point, and one which has a bearing on the value of correlational survey and laboratory experimental findings, is how to determine what is a stereotype. This is very basic question the answer to which is seldom sought by those who investigate the sex-stereotyping effects on television.

Research on viewers' perceptions of television characters is accumulating which indicates that the ways male and female actors are evaluated and described by viewers are determined by pre-existing beliefs and attitudes. Rather than being shaped by television, such beliefs and attitudes may pre-date and pre-determine preferences for and responses to television programmes (Gunter and Wober, 1982). This may occur even among young viewers. Reeves and Greenberg (1976) used multi-dimensional scaling techniques to explore the cognitive dimensions used by children in judging television characters. They found that boys focussed more on physical strength and activity attributes when describing characters, while girls were more likely to emphasize physical attractiveness. Reeves and Greenberg concluded that the dimensions identified are strong predictors of the children's desires to model the social behaviour of television characters behaving stereotypically. However, what these findings could indicate is that children come to television with already formed stereotypes and the fact that boys and girls used different terms to describe males and females, whether as seen on television or in real life, may have nothing to do directly with their experience with television sex-role portrayals.

The importance of other social forces in connection with reactions to television portrayals of the sexes was indicated in research by Williams et al (1981). Preconceptions about sex-appropriate traits and behaviours influenced children's ratings of male and female television actors. Further, children's beliefs that their own friends and peers in real life would approve of the way a particular character behaved was found to be an important determinant of their reported intentions to imitate or 'want to be with' that character. In line with the findings of Reeves and Greenberg reported above, Williams et al found that sex-typed biases in character perceptions seemed to rely as much on the sex of the viewer as on the sex of the character. Strength, for example, figured more prominently in the character preferences of boys than of girls. Likewise, 'good looks' was more important for girls than for boys, but also related well to the preferences of boys for female characters.

Among children and adults alike, attention to and liking for television characters may depend on whether viewers feel that their behaviour is altogether appropriate or acceptable to their particular sex, a judgement that is grounded in already well-formed opinions about sex roles. For instance, it has been observed that girls learn much less from a television news bulletin when the newscaster is a woman (Tan, Raudy, Huff & Miles 1980). And Durkin (1983) reported that young adult women tended to be much harsher in their evaluations of the reliability, qualifications, presentation skills and experience of a female weather forecaster than of a male weather forecaster. Young adult men, on the other hand, did not differ in their evaluations of the two forecasters.

Descriptive analyses of television portrayals of men and women may be relatively meaningless as indicators of the potential of television to cultivate sex-stereotyping when their schemes of programme content classification fail to take into account audience perceptions of character portrayals and social attitudinal norms which define what may currently be regarded as stereotyped or not. Research examining viewers' perceptions suggests that children's and adults' preferences for television characters and the way they behave are mediated by pre-existing beliefs concerning whether others in their social environment are likely to approve of those characters and their behaviours. If this evidence is reliable, then the quantities of males and females shown on television (something emphasised frequently by descriptive television content research) may be considerably less important than the qualities that are portrayed for each sex, and whether these qualities are perceived to be personally or socially acceptable.

The influence of television on sex-role attitudes and beliefs does not operate in a vacuum. The assumption embodied in so much research that television acts on passively receptive viewers to shape their behavioural dispositions or outlook on life is over-simplified and fails to tell the whole story. The study of television's influence needs instead to be put into a broader social and psychological context than has characterised most research to date, and considered alongside and in relation to other factors residing within individuals and the social environment in which they live.

References

Atkin, C., and Miller, M.M. (1975) *Experimental effects of television advertising on children.* Paper presented at the International Communication Association convention, Chicago, April.

Atwood, R.A., Zahn, S.B., and Webber, G. (1986) Perceptions of the traits of women on television. *Journal of Broadcasting,* **30,** 95-101.

Barcus, F.E. (1983) *Images of life on children's television: Sex roles, minorities and families.* New York: Praeger.

Bem, S. (1974) The measurement of psychological androgyny. *Journal of Consulting and Clinical Psychology,* **52,** 1551-62.

Bem, S. (1975) Sex role adaptability: One consequence of psychological androgyny. *Journal of Personality and Social Psychology.***31,** 634-643.

Bem, S. (1976) Probing the promise of androgyny. In A. Kaplan and J., Bean (Eds.), *Beyond sex-role .stereotypes: Reading towards a Psychology of androgyny.* Boston: Little, Brown.

Beuf, F.A. (1974) Doctor, Lawyer, Household drudge. *Journal of Communication,* **24,** 110-118.

Bronson, C.W. (1969) Sex differences in the development of fearfulness: A replication. *Psychonomic Science,* **17,** 367-368.

Busby, L.J. (1975) Sex role research on the mass media. *Journal of Communication,* **25,** 107-131.

Butler, M., and Paisley, W. (1980) *Women and the mass media.* New York: Human Sciences Press.

Cantor, M. (1979) Our days and nights on TV. *Journal of Communication,* **29,** 66-74.

Cathey-Calvert, C. (1983) *Sexisms of Sesame Street: outdated concepts in a progressive programme.* Pittsburgh Know. Inc.

Ceulemans, M., and Fauconnier, G. (1979) *Mass Media: The image, role and social conditions of women.* (Report No. 84). Paris, France: United Nations Educational, Scientific and Cultural Organisation.

Chappell, B. (1983) How women are portrayed in television commercials. *Admap,* June, 327-331.

Cheles-Miller, P. (1975) Restrictions to marital roles in commercials. *Journal of Advertising Research,* **15,** 45-49.

Chulay, C., and Francis, S. (1974) The image of the female child on Saturday morning television commercials. ERIC (ED 095603).

Clark, C. (1972) Race, identification and television violence, In C.A. Comstock, E.A. Rubinstein, and J.P. Murray (Eds.), *Television and social behaviour: Vol 5, Further explorations.* Washington, D.C.: U.S. Government Printing Office.

Cobb, N.J., Stevens-Long, J., and Goldstein, S. (1982) The influence of televised models on toy preference in children. *Sex Roles,* **5,** 1072-1080.

Courtney, A.E., and Whipple, T.W. (1975) Women in TV commercials. *Journal of Communication,* **24,** 110-118.

Davidson, E.S., Yasina, A., and Towers, A (1979) The effects of television cartoons on sex-role stereotyping in young girls. *Child Development,* **50,** 597-600.

De Charms, R. (1976) *Enhancing motivation change in the classroom.* New York: Irvington Publishers.

Dominick, J., and Rauch, G. (1971) The image of women in network TV commercials. *Journal of Broadcasting,* **16,** 259-265.

Downing, M. (1976) Heroine of the daytime serial. *Journal of Communication,* **24,** 130-139.

Drabman, R.S., Robertson, S.J., Patterson, J.N., Jarvie, G.J., Hammer, D., and Cordua, G. (1981) Children's perception of media-portrayed sex roles. *Sex Roles,* **12,** 379-389.

Durkin, K. (1983) *Sex roles and children's television,* A report to the Independent Broadcasting Authority. Social Psychology Research Unit, University of Kent, Canterbury.

Durkin, K. (1984) Children's accounts of sex-role stereotypes on television. *Communication Research,* **11,** 341-362.

Durkin, K. (1985a) Television and sex-role acquisition 1: Content *British Journal of Social Psychology.* **24,** 101-113.

Durkin, K. (1985b) Television and sex role acquisition 2: Effects. *British Journal of Social Psychology,* **24,** 211-222.

Durkin, K. (1985c) Television and sex-role acquisition 3: Counter-stereotyping. *British Journal of Social Psychology,* **24,** 211-222.

Fauls, L.B., and Smith, W.D. (1956) Sex-role learning in 5 year olds. *Journal of Genetic Psychology,* **89,** 195-117.

Feldstein, J.H., and Feldstein, S. (1982). Sex differences on televised toy commercials. *Sex Roles,* **8,** 581-587.

Flerx, V., Fidler, D., and Rogers, R. (1976) Sex role stereotypes: Development aspects and early intervention. *Child Development,* **47,** 998-1007.

Fagot, B.I., and Patterson, G.R. (1969) An *in vivo* analysis of reinforcing contingencies for sex-role behaviour in the preschool child. *Development Psychology,* 1, 563-568.

Freuh, T., and McGhee, P.E. (1975) Traditional sex-role development and amount of time spent watching television. *Developmental Psychology,* 11, 109.

Frieze, I.H., Parson, J.E., Johnson, P.B., Ruble, D.N., and Zellman, G.L. (1978) *Women and Sex roles: A social psychological perspective* New York Norton.

Furnham, A., and Schofield, S. (1986) Sex-role stereotyping in British radio advertisements. *British Journal of Social Psychology,* 25, 165-171.

Gallagher, M. (1983) *Why can't a man be more like a woman?* Report on the British component of a cross-cultural study of sex-role attitudes, perceptions and television viewing. Honolulu: East, West Centre, Institute of Culture and Communication.

Geis, F.L., Brown, V., Jennings (Walstedt), J., and Porter, N. TV commercials as achievement scripts for women. *Sex Roles,* 10, 513-525

Gerbner, G. (1972) Violence in television drama: Trends and symbolic functions. In G.A. Comstock and E.A. Rubinstein (Eds.), *Television and social behaviour, Vol 1, Content and control.* Washington, D.C.: U.S. Government Printing Office.

Gerbner, G., and Gross, L. (1976) Living with television. The violence profile. *Journal of Communication,* 26, 173-199.

Gerbner, G., and Signorielli, N. (1979) *Women and minorities in television drama: 1969-1978: Research report.* Annenberg School of Communications, Philadelphia, in collaboration with the Seven Actors Guild, AFL-C10 October 29.

Goff, D.H., Goff, L.D., and Lehrer, S.K. (1980) Sex-role portrayals of selected female television characters. *Journal of Broadcasting,* 24, 467-475.

Greenberg, B., Richards, M., and Henderson, L. (1980) Trends in sex-role portrayals on television. In B. Greenberg (Ed.), *Life on television,* Norwood, N.J.: Ablex Press.

Grusec, J.E., and Brinker, D.B. (1972) Reinforcement for imitation as a social learning determinant with implications for sex role development. *Journal of Personality and Social Psychology,* 21, 149-158.

Gunter, B. (1984) *TV viewing and perceptions of men and women on TV and in real life.* London: Independent Broadcasting Authority, Research paper, September.

Gunter, B., and Wober, M. (1982) Television viewing and perceptions of women on TV and in real life. *Current Psychological Research,* 2, 277-288.

Harris, P.R., and Stobart, J. (1986) Sex-role stereotyping in British television advertisements at different times of the day: An extension and refinement of Manstead & McCulloch (1981). *British Journal of Social Psychology,* 25, 155-164.

Hawkins, R., and Pingree, S. (1982) Television's influence on social reality. In D. Pearl, L. Bouthilet and J. Lazar (Eds.) *Television and behaviour: Ten years of scientific progress and implications for the eighties.* Rockville, Maryland, Institute of Mental Health.

Head, H. (1954) Content analysis of television drama programmes. *Quarterly of Film, Radio and Television,* **9,** 175-194.

Hennessee, J., and Nicholson, J. (1972) NOW says: TV commercials insult women. *New York Times Magazine,* May 28, PP13, 48-51.

Hodges, K.K., Brandt, D.A., and Kline, J. (1981) Competence, guilt and victimization: Sex differences in ambition of causality in television dramas. *Sex Roles,* **7,** 537-546.

Jennings, J., Geis, F.L., and Brown, V. (1980) Influence of television on women's self-confidence and independent judgement. *Journal of Personality and Social Psychology,* **38,** 203-210.

Johnson, J., and Ettema, J.S. (1982) *Positive Images.* Beverly Hills: Sage.

Joy, L., Kimball, M., and Zabrock, M. (1977) *Television exposure and children's aggressive behaviour.* Paper presented at the meeting of the Canadian Psychological Association, Vancouver, June.

Katzman, N. (1972) Television soap operas: What's been going on anyway? *Public Opinion Quarterly,* **36,** 200-212.

Kimball, M. (1986) Television and sex-role attitudes. In T.M. Williams (Ed.), *The Impact of Television,* London: Academic Press.

Knill, B.J., Peach, M., Pursey, G., Gilpin, P. and Perloff, R.M. (1981) Still typecast after all these years: Sex role portrayals in television advertising. *International Journal of Women's Studies,* **4,** 497-506.

Kohlberg, L.A. (1966) Cognitive developmental analysis of children's sex role concepts and attitudes. In E. Maccoby (Ed.) *The development of sex differences. Stanford Calif.: Stanford University Press.*

Lemon, J. (1977) Women and blacks on prime-time television. *Journal of Communication.* **27,** 70-74.

Levinson, R. (1975) From Olive Oyl to Sweet Polly Purebread: Sex role stereotypes and televised cartoons. *Journal of Popular Culture,* **9,** 561-572.

Livingstone, S., and Green, G. (1986) Television advertisements and the portrayal of gender. *British Journal of Social Psychology,* **25,** 149-154.

Long, M., and Simon, R. (1974) The roles and statuses of women and children on family TV programmes. *Journalism Quarterly,* **51,** 107-110.

Maccoby, E.E., and Jacklin, C.N. (1973) *The psychology of sex differences,* Stanford, CA.,: Stanford University Press.

Maccoby, E.E., and Wilson, W.C. (1957) Identification and observational learning from films. *Journal of Abnormal and Social Psychology,* **55,** 76-87.

Maracek, J., Piliavin, J.A., Fitzsimmons, E., Krogh, E.C., Leader, E., and Trudell, B. (1976) Women as TV experts: The voice of authority? *Journal of Communication,* **28,** 159-168.

Manstead, A.R.S., and McCulloch, C. (1981) Sex role stereotyping in British television advertisements. *British Journal of Social Psychology,* **20,** 171-180.

Manes, A.l., and Melnyk, P. (1974) Televised models of female achievement. *Journal of Applied Social Psychology,* **4,** 365-374.

Mayes, S.L., and Valentine, K.B. (1979) Sex role stereotyping in Saturday morning cartoon shows. *Journal of Broadcasting,* **23,** 41-50.

McArthur, L.Z., and Eisen, S. (1976) Achievements of male and female storybook characters as determinants of achievement behaviour in boys and girls. *Journal of Personality and Social Psychology, 33,* 467-473.

McArthur, L.Z., and Resko, B.G. (1975) The portrayal of men and women in American television commercials. *Journal of Social Psychology, 97,* 209-220.

McGhee, P.E. (1975) Television as a source of learning sex-role stereotypes. In S. Cohen and T.J. Comiskey (Eds) *Child Development: Contemporary perspectives,* Ithace, IL: Pencock Publichers.

McGhee, P., and Frueh, T. (1980) Television viewing and the learning of sex-role stereotypes. *Sex Roles, 2,* 179-188.

McNeil, J. (1975) Feminism, femininity and the television shows: A content analysis. *Journal of Broadcasting, 19,* 259-269.

Meyer, B. (1980) The development of girls' sex-role attitudes. *Child Development, 51,* 508-514.

Miles, B. (1975) *Channelling children: sex stereotyping as primetime TV.* Princeton, N.J.: Women on Words and Images.

Mischel, W. (1966) A social learning view of sex differences in behaviour. In E. Maccoby (Ed.) *The development of sex differences.* Stanford, Calif.: Stanford University Press.

Miller, M., and Reeves, B. (1976) Dramatic TV content and children's sex-role stereotypes. *Journal of Broadcasting, 20,* 35-50.

Mischel, W. (1970) A social learning view of sex differences in behaviour. In P.H. Mussen (Ed.) *Carmichael's Manual of Child Psychology,* New York: Wiley.

Morgan, M. (1982) Television and adolescents' sex role stereotypes: A longitudinal study. *Journal of Personality and Social Psychology, 43,* 947-955.

Nolan, J.D., J.P., and White, M.A. (1977) Sex bias on children's television programmes. *Journal of Psychology, 96,* 197-204.

O'Donnell, W.J., and O'Donnell, K.J. (1978) Update: sex role messages in TV commercials. *Journal of Broadcasting, 28,* 156-158.

O'Kelly, C.G., and Bloomqvist, L.E. (1976) Women and blacks on TV. *Journal of Communication, 26,* 179-192.

Peevers, B.H., (1979) Androgyny on the TV screen? An analysis of sex role portrayals. *Sex Roles, 5,* 797-809.

Perloff, R.M. (1977) Some antecedents of children's sex-role stereotypes. *Psychological Reports, 40,* 436-466.

Perloff, R., Brown, J., and Miller, M. (1982) Mass media and sex-typing: Research perspectives and policy implications. *International Journal of Women's Studies, 5,* 265-273.

Pingree, S. (1978) The effects of nonsexist television commercials and perceptions of reality on children's attitudes about women. *Psychology of Women Quarterly, 2,* 262-276.

Reeves, B., and Greenberg, B. (1976) Children's perceptions of television characters. *Human Communication Research, 3,* 113-127.

Rosencrantz, P., Vogel, S., Bee, H., Broverman, I., and Broverman, D. (1968)

Sex-role stereotypes and self-concepts in college students. *Journal of Consulting and Clinical Psychology,* **32,** 287-295.

Schechtman, S.A. (1978) Occupational portrayal of men and women on the most frequently mentioned television shows of pre-school children. *Resource in Education,* (ERIC Document Reproduction Service N.ED 174-156).

Scheibe, C. (1979) Sex roles in TV commercials. *Journal of Advertising Research,* **19,** 23-28.

Schneider, K.C. (1979) Sex roles in television commercials: new dimensions for comparison. *Akron Business and Economic Review,* **Fall,** 20-24.

Schwartz, L. (1974) The image of women in the novels of Mme. de Souza. *The University of Michigan Papers in Women's Studies,* **I,** 142-148.

Seggar, J.F., Hafen, J.K., and Hannonen-Gladden, H. (1981) Television's portrayals of minorities and women in drama and comedy drama: 1971-80. *Journal of Broadcasting,* **25,** 277-288.

Seggar, J., and Wheeler, P. (1973) World of work on TV: Ethnic and sex representation in TV drama. *Journal of Broadcasting,* **17,** 201-214.

Sharits, N., and Lammers, B.H., (1983) Perceived attributes of models in prime-time and daytime television commercials: A person perception approach. *Journal of Marketing Research,* **20,** 64-73.

Sherman, J.A. (1971) *On the psychology of women.* Springfield, IL.: Charles Thomas.

Signorielli, N. (1984) The demography of the television world. In G. Melischeck, K.E. Rosengren, and J. Stappers (Eds.), *Cultural Indicators: An international symposium.* Vienna, Austria. Austrian Academy of Sciences.

Singer, J.L., and Singer, D.G. (1981) *Television, imagination and aggression: A study of preschoolers.* Hillsdale, N.J.: Lawrence Erlbaum Associates.

Spiegler, M.D. and Liebert, R.M. (1970) Some correlates of self-reported fear. *Psychological Reporter,* **26,** 691-695.

Silverstein, A., and Silverstein, R. (1974) The portrayal of women in television advertising. *Federal Communications Bar Journal,* **27,** 71-98.

Smythe, D.W. (1954) Reality as presented by television. *Public Opinion Quarterly,* **18,** 143-154.

Sprafkin, M. and Liebert, R.M. (1978) sex-typing and children's preferences. In G. Techman, A. Daniels and J. Benet (Eds) *Health and Home: Images of women in the mass media* New York, Oxford University Press. 288-339.

Stern, D.N. and Bender, E.P. (1974) An ethological study of children approaching a strange adult: Sex differences. In R.C. Friedman, R.M. Richards, R.L. Vand Wiele and L.D. Stern (Eds) *Sex Differences in Children* (New York Wiley).

Spence, J.T., Helmreich, R., and Strapp, J. (1975) Ratings of self and peers on sex-role attitudes and their relation to self-esteem and conception of masculinity and femininity. *Journal of Personality and Social Psychology.* **32,** 20-39.

Sternglanz, S., and Serbin, L. (1974) Sex role stereotyping on children's television programmes. *Developmental Psychology,* **10,** 710-715.

Tan, A. (1979) TV beauty ads and role expectations of adolescent female viewers. *Journalism Quarterly,* **56,** 283-288.

Tan, A., Raudy, J., Huff, C., and Miles, J. (1980) Children's reactions to male and female newscasters' effectiveness and believability. *Quarterly Journal of Speech,* **66,** 201-205.

Tedesco, N. (1974) Patterns in prime-time. *Journal of Communication,* **74,** 119-124.

Tuchman, G. (1978) The symbolic annihilation of women by the mass media. In G. Tuchman, A. Daniels, and J. Benet, (Eds.) *Hearth and home: Images of women in the mass media.* New York: Oxford University Press.

Turner, M.E. (1974) Sex role attitudes and fear of success in relation to achievement behaviour in women. *Dissertation Abstracts International* **35,** 5-B), 2451-2452.

Turow, J. (1974) Advising and ordering: Daytime, prime time. *Journal of Communication,* **24,** 135-141.

Verna, M.E. (1975) The female image in children's TV commercials. *Journal of Broadcasting,* **19,** 301-309.

Volgy, J.J., and Schwartz, J.E. (1980) TV entertainment programming and socio-political attitudes, *Journalism Quarterly,* **57,** 150-155.

Welch, R.L., Huston-Stein, A., Wright, J.C., and Plehal, R. (1979) Subtle sex-role cues in children's commercials. *Journal of Communication,* **29,** 202-209.

Williams, F., La Rose, R., and Frost, F. (1981) *Children, television and sex-role stereotyping.* New York: Praeger.

Williams, T.M. (1986) *The Impact of Television,* London: Academic Press.

Wilson, G.D. (1966) An electrodermal technique for the study of phobia. *New England Medical Journal,* **85,** 696-698.

Wilson, G.D. (1967) Social desirability and sex differences in expressed fear. *Behaviour Research and Therapy,* **5,** 136-137.

Winick, C., Williamson, L.G., Chuzmir, S.F., and Winick, M.P. (1973) *Children's Television Commercials: A Content Analysis.* New York: Praeger.

Zuckerman, D.M., Singer, D.G., and Singer, J.L. (1980) Children's television viewing, racial and sex role attitudes. *Journal of Applied Psychology,* **10,** 281-294.